MIAMI
IN OUR OWN WORDS

MIAMI
IN OUR OWN WORDS

BY THE STAFF OF THE MIAMI HERALD

PHOTOGRAPHY BY C.W. GRIFFIN

EDITED BY NANCY ANCRUM AND RICH BARD

THE MIAMI HERALD

ANDREWS AND McMEEL
A UNIVERSAL PRESS SYNDICATE COMPANY
KANSAS CITY

Miami: In Our Own Words © 1995 by The Miami Herald. All rights reserved. Printed in the United States of America. No part of this book may be used or reproduced in any manner whatsoever without the written permission of Andrews and McMeel except in the case of reprints in the context of reviews. For information, write Andrews and McMeel, a Universal Press Syndicate Company, 4900 Main Street, Kansas City, Missouri 64112.

Additional copies of this book may be ordered by calling (800) 642-6480.

Library of Congress Cataloging-in-Publication Data

Miami : in our own words / by the staff of the Miami herald ; photography by C.W. Griffin ; edited by Nancy Ancrum and Rich Bard.
    p. cm.
  ISBN 0-8362-0572-3 (paper)
  1. Miami (Fla.)—History. 2. Miami (Fla.)—Social life and customs. 3. Miami (Fla.)—Biography. 4. Interviews—Florida—Miami. I. Griffin, C. W. II. Ancrum, Nancy. III. Bard, Rich. IV. Miami herald (Miami, Fla.)
F319.M6M6355   1995
975.9'381—dc20   95-20600
                                                                                                             CIP

CONTENTS

Acknowledgments 6
Foreword by David Lawrence Jr. 8

I. ORANGE BLOSSOMS, BIG WINDS, AND REFUGE SEEKERS
Miami Milestones, 1513–1995
Timeline
  by William Robertson 12

II. BOATS, PLANES, TRAINS — AND A TOUCHDOWN
Now Is the Time
Historians 20
Sammy and Ruthie Charin
  (Interview by Marilyn Adams) 22
Irving Fryar
  (Interview by Armando Salguero) 24
Herbert Karliner
  (Interview by John Lantigua) 27
June Taylor
  (Interview by Jane Wooldridge) 30
Elly Chovel
  (Interview by Liz Balmaseda) 33
Nguyen Van Luc
  (Interview by Al Topping) 37

III. BUGS, BIRDS, BOUGAINVILLEA — AND A SWAMP
The Nature of This Place
Historians 40
Janet Reno
  (Interview by Martha Musgrove) 42
Gilbert Clark
  (Interview by Arnold Markowitz) 45
Mort Cooper
  (Interview by Richard Wallace) 48
Dina Knapp
  (Interview by Nancy Ancrum) 52
Capt. Bob Lewis
  (Interview by Arnold Markowitz) 54

IV. PIONEERS AND BRICKLAYERS
Laying Miami's Foundations
Historians 58
Marjory Stoneman Douglas
  (Interview and compilation
  by Geoffrey Tomb) 60
Stetson Kennedy
  (Interview by William Robertson) 64
Morris Lapidus
  (Interview by Jo Werne) 68
Judy Drucker
  (Interview by Gail Meadows) 71
William Krome Jr.
  (Interview by Kathleen Krog) 75
Maurice Ferre
  (Interview by Rick Hirsch) 79
Dr. Jean Jones Perdue
  (Interview by Nancy Ancrum) 83

V. PSALMS, SONGS, AND SALVATION
Sustaining the Spirit
Historians 88
Gian Carlo Vacchelli
  (Interview by Jon O'Neill) 90
Luciano Garcia
  (Interview by Cynthia Corzo) 94
Roxcy Bolton
  (Interview by Bill Rose) 98
Dr. John O. Brown
  (Interview by Tananarive Due) 101
Mark King Leban
  (Interview by Sam Terilli) 105
Haydee Marin
  (Interview by Maria Morales) 108
Monsignor Bryan Walsh
  (Interview by Grace Lim) 111
Glenn Terry
  (Interview by Dave Barry) 115

VI. BEHIND THE BADGE, ON THE BENCH, FROM THE DAIS
Politics and the Law
Historians 120
Arnold Gibbs
  (Interview by Gail Epstein) 122
Tom Cash
  (Interview by Jeff Leen) 126
Shelley Kravitz
  (Interview by Jo Werne) 130
Dante Fascell
  (Interview by Tom Fiedler) 134
Xavier Suarez
  (Interview by John Pancake) 138
Jose Enrique Dauza
  (Interview by Olga Connor) 142

VII. STAKING A CLAIM, MAKING A BUCK, STRIKING IT RICH
The Art of Enterprise
Historians 146
Edwin Stephan
  (Interview by Ted Reed) 148
The Women of the S&S
  (Interview by Larry Meyer) 152
Haydee and Sahara Scull
  (Interview by Norma Niurka) 156
Joenel Ceremy
  (Interview by Jacqueline Charles) 160
Teo Babun
  (Interview by Armando Correa) 162
Rev. Dennis Tarr
  (Interview by Tony Proscio) 166
Alvino Monk
  (Interview by Susana Barciela) 170
Ellen Johnson
  (Interview by Jacqui Love Marshall) 174

VIII. THE FRUITS OF DEEP ROOTS, A SENSE OF COMMUNITY
Thriving on Our Heritage
Historians 178
Bob Kaufman
  (Interview by Bob Kearney) 180
Denise Wallace
  (Interview by John Barry) 182
Robert Lamme
  (Interview by Pat May) 186
Alicia Baro (Interview by Bea Moss) 189
Enid Pinkney
  (Interview by Tony Pugh) 193
Drs. Pedro Jose Greer
  (Interview by Rosa Bautista) 197
Susie Jim Billie
  (Interview by Carl Hiaasen) 201

ACKNOWLEDGMENTS

Nancy Ancrum, a member of the *Herald* editorial board, has worked for the *Herald* for 12 years. A New York native, she is a graduate of New York University. She was an editor at the *Evening Sun* in Baltimore and *USA Today* before coming to the *Herald*. She lives in Miami Shores with her husband, George Fishman, and two dogs.

Rich Bard is Sunday Viewpoint editor of the *Herald*, where he has worked for 20 years. He was born and raised in Oklahoma City. He earned a master's degree in political science from the University of Oklahoma and was a journalism fellow at Duke University. He and his wife, Karen, have two children. Bard is on the board of Pinecrest Presbyterian Church.

Photographer C.W. Griffin has been at the *Herald* for 12 years. His photographs have been published in a variety of books, including *Songs of My People*, *A Day in the Life of Israel*, and *The African-Americans*. A veteran of the U.S. Navy, he is the only African American to be named Military Photographer of the Year, an honor he received in 1981.

ABOUT THIS BOOK

Don't be fooled by the paperbound nature of *Miami: In Our Own Words*. This city's history does not lie lifeless on the pages of some book. Miami's first 100 years are a living, breathing record of pioneering verve and clear-eyed vision. Many of the foundation builders are still with us—a major advantage of a city this young. They have been joined through the years by thousands of freedom seekers, sun lovers, and people looking to start over—all of whom have stories to tell.

They are the engine driving *Miami: In Our Own Words*. On these pages are the memories and experiences of a community, as told by the people who live them. Word for word, these are their words.

This book represents an all-volunteer effort from throughout the *Herald*. Dozens of staffers conducted taped interviews with each subject, whose stories were transcribed, then edited for book presentation. The final version of each interview was limited solely by space parameters. However, each was edited with a careful eye toward preserving—and highlighting—the cadence, the lyricism, the force of each person's speaking. (Take a look at Stetson Kennedy's interview—you'll see what we mean.) Each is accompanied by a compelling, evocative portrait that brings each speaker to life.

There are myriad *Herald* people who played an important role in bringing this book itself to life. Among them are the members of the *Herald*'s Centennial Task Force, led by Larry Meyer, executive assistant to the publisher, and Betty Grudzinski, who shepherded this project to published form.

In addition, special thanks to William Robertson, who compiled the "Miami Milestones" time line, designer Steve Rice, translator Renato Perez, and researcher Lillian Osorio for executing these "volunteer" tasks while doing their daily jobs, too.

If the storytellers were this book's engine, then Randy Nimnicht, president of the Historical Museum of Southern Florida, provided the map that was followed. He gave unselfishly of his time, erecting guideposts—and warning of potholes—that brought this project to fruition.

SPECIAL THANKS
The editors give their warmest thanks to these people for their invaluable assistance:

Herald Task Force members: Sharon Clark, Richard DeQuattro, Susan Kelly-Gilbert, Carolyn Lavan, Silvia Licha, Lynn Medford, Susan Olds, Leonard Reynolds, Maria Smith, Bill Whiting, Nery Ynclan.

Also: Reg Bragonier, Natalie Brown, Dr. Juan Clark, Doug Clifton, Opal Comfort, Olga Connor, Glenna Cook-McKitterick, Dennis Copeland, Eliana de Marcos, Elly du Pré, T. Willard Fair;

Dorothy Jenkins Fields, George Fishman, Dr. Paul George, Jennifer Gonzalez, Phil and Penny Green, Martha Hubbard, Jim Karousatos, Sallye Jude, Margaret Kempel, Saundra Keyes, Howard Kleinberg, Cathy Leff;

Elisabeth B. Lilly, Jesus Mendez, Gene Miller, Luzy Natal, Joe Natoli, Ileana Oroza, Arva Moore Parks, Mark Reeves;

Dr. Sharyn Richardson, Mark Robinson, Chris Rollins, Kathy Fernandez Rundle, Rebecca Smith, Randy Stano, Roberto Suarez, Winston Townsend, Battle Vaughan.

FOREWORD

Enter the *Herald*'s main newsroom, and you will pass a photograph that conveys just how far our resilient, sun-bronzed city has come in such a short time. Taken in 1910, the year the *Miami Morning News-Record* became the *Miami Herald*, the photograph shows three pressmen posing with a single Goss Comet press. Two in front, both white, wear white shirts and ties; an African American stands in the back.

Well worth wondering is what those pressmen, toiling indoors in the subtropical heat, would have said about a city then no older than a teenager. Their Miami was vastly different from the air-conditioned, cyberspace, pulsing stew of a metropolis its current inhabitants know. The pressmen's tales, had they been recorded beyond the instant of that photo, are a part of Miami history as valid as, let us say, the great hurricane of 1926, the exile exodus beginning in 1959 or the Dolphins' perfect 1972 season.

Every one of us has a story to tell. All of us—native and newcomer, banker and bank thief, homemaker and homeboy, exile and ex-Iowan, cracker and Cuban and Haitian and a multitude more—have a valuable perspective.

Each of us contributes at least a stitch to the whole cloth of Greater Miami's history.

It is a short arc, 100 years, on the timeline of recorded history. But in that blink of time, beginning July 28, 1896, when the village growing along the Miami River was incorporated, we have become no less than a global city of the future. We commit to life here knowing it requires more understanding than most places.

Living here, amid the passion and the anxiety and the tedium (and yes, the heat those pressmen endured), we share the chance to be that history—and to become so much more.

In celebrating a century of becoming a city, then, the *Herald* compiled dozens of oral histories—individual snippets of a place, a time, a people—and compiled them into this volume. The audio tapes, to be archived in appropriate repositories around town, will become part of the legacy of the centennial year.

What emerges is proof that this is a whirlygig town of individuals, each with warts-and-all biases, each with stories that bind us as a community. You will discover within these pages a friend, a neighbor, or simply a reflection of yourself.

In that way, *Miami: In Our Own Words* becomes not just a chronicle of days gone by, but a catalyst for how we live and how, together, we look to the future. This is the place of the great American adventure. This is the future.

Let us go forth. *Adelante*.

Dave Lawrence

ORANGE BLOSSOMS, BIG WINDS, AND REFUGE SEEKERS

HIGHLIGHTING MIAMI'S HISTORY

MIAMI MILESTONES
1513-1995

BY WILLIAM ROBERTSON

1513—The conquistador Juan Ponce de Leon lands somewhere on the upper east coast of the Florida peninsula.

1825—The U.S. government builds the lighthouse at Cape Florida, on Key Biscayne.

1836—Seminole Indians attack a plantation on the New River. A slave escapes and warns the settlement at Cape Florida that the Indians are coming. Most of the settlers leave for Key West, but the acting Cape Florida lighthouse keeper, John Thompson, and his assistant, Aaron Carter, remain. The Indians set fire to the structure and leave the two men for dead. Carter dies. Thompson is rescued by sailors.

1837—As protection against the Seminoles, the U.S. begins building Fort Dallas.

1842—Miami first receives its name as William H. English plats the "Village of Miami."

1846—The Cape Florida lighthouse is rebuilt.

1856—During the Third Seminole War (1855-57), U.S. Army Lt. Abner Doubleday, who will later be credited with inventing baseball, supervises construction of a road between Miami and Fort Lauderdale.

1861–65—The Civil War years find Miami a place with sympathizers of both sides. At the war's end, a Union gunboat arrives at

IN MIAMI'S BIRTH YEAR: Ground is broken March 15, 1896, for the Royal Palm Hotel, across the river from the Brickell Trading Post.

Key Biscayne to thwart the attempts of any Southern officials to flee the country. Despite the Union presence, Confederate Treasury Secretary John Breckenridge escapes through Miami.

1865—The Freedman's Bureau surveys South Florida as a possible place to resettle 50,000 former slaves, but the plan falls through.

1870—Two new pioneers arrive from Cleveland. They are William H. Brickell and Ephraim T. Sturtevant, father of Julia Tuttle. The names Brickell and Tuttle will become almost synonymous with Miami.

1881—Brothers Charles and Jack Peacock build Miami's first public lodging in what will become Coconut Grove.

1891—Julia Tuttle moves from Cleveland to Miami and buys an extensive tract of land on the north side of the Miami River. She has a vision of Miami as a prosperous city. She promises she will give half of her land to anyone who will build a railroad to Miami. She approaches Henry Flagler, who is extending his rail line to Palm Beach. Initially, Flagler is not interested. But in the winter of 1894–95, a freeze devastates the citrus crop in Central Florida. Tuttle points out to Flagler that the cold has not reached South Florida. She offers him half her land if he will extend his rail line. Storekeeper and Indian trader William Brickell

MILESTONES

JULIA TUTTLE

offers Flagler some of his land south of the river. Flagler is convinced.

1896—On April 22, the first passenger train reaches Miami. On July 28, 344 voters agree to incorporate Miami as a city. But it almost dies in the year of its birth. On Christmas night, a fire incinerates 28 buildings.

1897—Henry Flagler's majestic Royal Palm Hotel, with 350 guest rooms, opens.

1898—The U.S.S. Maine is blown up at Havana, triggering war with Spain. Some 7,000 U.S. troops arrive in Miami. During their stay, the bored soldiers, encamped in the summer heat and beset by mosquitoes, terrify the community. Julia Tuttle dies at 49.

1899—Miami is quarantined for three months after a yellow fever outbreak.

1905—Tourists continue to visit Miami, and new hotels are built to accommodate them. The city features several movie theaters, some with canvas roofs that can be rolled back to allow in the breeze. The bayshore is bustling with boats. A ferry shuttles bathers to the oceanfront on what will become Miami Beach. Flagler begins building the railroad to Key West, opening up South Dade to large farms that send vegetables to the north in winter. A speed limit advises drivers to go no faster than 8 mph.

1909—Habitable land in South Florida is on a limestone ridge about four miles wide. To the west are sawgrass swamps; on the east are mangrove swamps. This will soon change as engineers begin digging the Miami Canal to drain the Everglades at the edge of the city. Even at this early stage in Miami's development, some conservationists exist: The Florida Federation of Women's Clubs seeks to preserve the Everglades, eventually acquiring (in 1916) 4,000 acres.

1912—Supervised by engineer William J. Krome, Henry Flagler's railroad reaches Key West. A year later Flagler dies in Palm Beach at 83.

HENRY FLAGLER

1913—Pioneer John Collins, with financial help from Carl Fisher, opens a bridge from the mainland to Miami Beach. Fisher clears the island of mangroves and dredges sand from Biscayne Bay to create dry land. On the other side of Biscayne Bay, Miami is promoted heavily by merchant E.G. Sewell. Among Sewell's showier accomplishments: He brings the first airplane to Miami; he convinces pioneer aviator Glenn Curtiss to open a flying school; he conducts a national advertising campaign— Miami's first—to lure tourists. Among the rich and famous wintering in Miami: James Deering, a manufacturer of farming equipment, who will build the city's most spectacular mansion, Villa Vizcaya. As white Miami grows, a separate black community is grow-

MILESTONES

ing with it, in pockets at Coconut Grove, Lemon City and "Colored Town," later to be called Overtown, a thriving business district.

1914—Joe and Jennie Weiss operate a restaurant in their home on Miami Beach—later to be called Joe's Stone Crab.

1915—Miami Beach is incorporated.

1917—The nation enters World War I. On the home front, the Navy operates a flying school in Coconut Grove. At Dinner Key Naval Air Station, 128 seaplanes are moored. An Army school opens in Cutler, and Glenn Curtiss trains Marine pilots.

1918—In October, the flu epidemic, which claims millions of lives across America, reaches Miami. In November the war ends, and Miami is on the cusp of the Roaring Twenties.

1920–25—The expansion of Miami overwhelms its pattern of street names and the city council approves a new grid system. Ground zero is at the newly named Flagler Street and Miami Avenue. The city's skyline continues to rise. A bayfront park is created by dredging. Real estate speculation is an obsession and the town is filled with promoters both legitimate and shady. Another developer with a vision, George Merrick, creates Coral Gables. He hires the fabled politician and orator William Jennings Bryan to give promotional lectures. Speculation by now is out of control. The national news media, as it will again and again, declare that all is not well in paradise and that investing in Florida real estate is risky. Sales begin to dwindle and the party is winding down.

1926—In September, South Floridians are warned of an approaching hurricane. It will become part of Miami legend. The last gauge to stay in place records winds of 128 mph. When the winds subside and the seas recede, little is left of the city. Despite their desperation, Miamians begin rebuilding immediately. The University of Miami finally opens in makeshift quarters. Enough reconstruction takes place to host a tourist season. The city develops an esprit and sense of community unlike any it will see for 66 more years, when Hurricane Andrew devastates South Dade.

In Cuba's Oriente province, a son is born to Angel Castro y Argiz and Lina Ruiz Gonzalez. They name the child Fidel.

1927—Pan American Airways contracts to fly mail between Key West and Havana. The airline will soon make Miami the U.S. point of departure for Latin America. Pan Am's field will become Miami International Airport.

1928—Tamiami Trail is completed, connecting Miami with Florida's west coast. Prohibition is on and, with its hidden inlets, creeks and canals, Miami earns a reputation as a paradise for bootleggers. Gambling is rampant. Gangster Al Capone moves to Palm Island. A hurricane spares Miami but hits Palm Beach County, killing 1,800.

1930—The Great Depression takes its relentless toll. Still, all isn't gloom. A new airline named Eastern, run by Eddie Rickenbacker, begins the first passenger service between South Florida and the North.

1933—President-elect Franklin Delano Roosevelt visits Miami. At Bayfront Park, a disgruntled brick mason, Guiseppe Zangara, tries to assassinate him. Zangara misses Roosevelt, but fatally wounds Chicago Mayor Anton Cermak.

1935—Miami is spared the wrath of a hurricane, but not the Keys. The storm comes ashore in the Upper Keys with winds of 250 mph. Virtually nothing is left standing; at least 500 die.

1936—The first Orange Bowl Parade marches through downtown. Pan American Airways has

MILESTONES

moved its terminal to Dinner Key and Eastern Airlines has taken over the inland Pan Am field. Miami shows signs of recovering from the Depression as the number of tourists increases, including many from Latin America. Some stores post signs in Spanish. The song "Moon Over Miami" tops the hit parade. In the next few years, Art Deco buildings change the look of Miami Beach.

1940—England is already at war with Germany and sends a contingent of Royal Air Force pilots to train at the University of Miami and Pan American Airways.

1941—The Japanese bomb Pearl Harbor, bringing the United States into World War II. Miami Beach quickly becomes a military training center.

1942—German submarines operate brazenly off the Florida coast. U-boats torpedo 25 ships between Key West and Cape Canaveral. Four are seen by Miamians. Residents fear an attack on Miami Beach. Operating out of Miami, Navy patrols, aided by blimps, hunt down the subs and gradually chase them out of Florida waters. Not before, however, one blimp is shot down by a sub.

1945—The war is coming to a close, but a conflict closer to home begins. Blacks attempt a swim-in at the beach at Baker's Haulover. The county soon opens the beach at Virginia Key for blacks only, accessible only by ferry. The causeway will not be finished until 1947.

1946—A postwar boom begins as veterans who trained in Miami decide to return to live. Between 1940 and 1950, the population doubles. The University of Miami is filled with veterans. Heavy rains from back-to-back storms in 1947 leave Miami flooded, and new engineering plans are drawn to dry up the Everglades. President Harry Truman opens Everglades National Park.

1949—The first television station in Florida, WTVJ, begins broadcasting.

1950—Miami has become a mecca for organized crime in the postwar years. Illegal gambling is rampant. U.S. Sen. Estes Kefauver comes to town to hold televised hearings on crime.

1951—A black housing project, Carver Village, is bombed, and the first Council for Human Relations is formed. A year later Dade County Auditorium is integrated after opera singer Marian Anderson refuses to perform before a segregated audience.

1953—Radio and television personality Arthur Godfrey brings his popular variety show to Miami Beach, touting the region's charm to the nation. A hotel building boom transforms Miami Beach. Miami is well on its way to becoming the vacation destination of choice for millions of Americans. Miami's destiny, however, is being shaped elsewhere. In Cuba, Castro leads an abortive attack on the Moncada army barracks in Santiago.

1956—Castro uses the Sierra Maestra mountains from which to wage a guerrilla revolutionary war.

1957—Metropolitan government is created in Dade County under a Home Rule Charter.

1959—Castro topples the government of Fulgencio Batista.

1960—At first embraced as Cuba's new hope, the Castro regime grows ever more brutal, and a trickle of refugees turns into a flood. Destination: Miami.

1961—A brigade of exiles lands in Cuba at the Bay of Pigs to reclaim their homeland from Castro. More than 1,000 men of Brigade 2506 are taken prisoner.

1962—The U.S. discovers that the Soviet Union is using Cuba as a missile base. President John F. Kennedy orders a naval blockade and demands that the missiles be removed. Miami and the Keys

MILESTONES

become a military staging area as fears of war grow. Soviet leader Nikita Khrushchev blinks and promises to remove the missiles in return for a U.S. pledge not to invade Cuba. Years later, those in the president's inner circle will say that never has the world been so close to nuclear war. Kennedy agrees to ransom the Bay of Pigs prisoners for $62 million in medical supplies and food, then welcomes them at a ceremony in the Orange Bowl.

1964—In Miami Beach, Cassius Clay (later Muhammad Ali) knocks out Sonny Liston to win the world heavyweight boxing title. The Beatles make their first American TV appearance on "The Ed Sullivan Show," broadcast from Miami Beach.

1965—The Freedom Flights begin to bring refugees from Cuba to the United States. By the time the flights end in 1973, they will have brought in 150,000 exiles.

1968—At the height of the turbulent '60s, the Republicans hold their national convention in Miami Beach and nominate Richard Nixon, who has a home on Key Biscayne, as their presidential candidate. As television beams the convention across the country, Miami experiences its first racial riot. The Liberty City upheaval

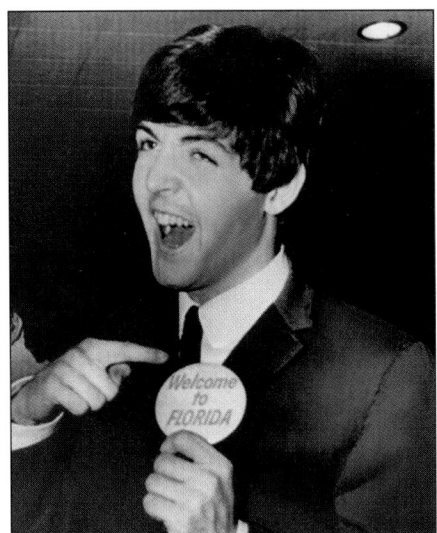

THE BEATLES COME TO AMERICA: Paul McCartney of the Beatles displays his "Welcome to Florida" button during the Beatles' 1964 visit to Miami. They made their first U.S. TV appearance on the "Ed Sullivan Show," broadcast from Miami Beach. (Photo by John Pineda)

occurs despite the 1964 Civil Rights Act, which has ended legal segregation and given blacks a political voice. As one result, Miami has elected its first black, Athalie Range, to the City Commission.

1969—As the decade nears its close, Miami can look back not only on turmoil. The '60s have seen the opening of Miami-Dade Junior College, the coming of professional football with the Miami Dolphins, the population increase to one million and a series of environmental initiatives that have created John Pennekamp State Park in Key Largo, Biscayne National Monument in the south bay and Bill Baggs-Cape Florida State Park on Key Biscayne.

1970—Federal Judge C. Clyde Atkins orders Dade County teachers integrated.

1972—Florida International University opens.

1975—A recession is taking its toll on the city. Construction has virtually stopped. Other changes are more subtle. Cuban exiles, who still dream of returning to Cuba, are becoming integrated into the life of the city, giving it an international identity.

1977—The unimaginable happens: It snows in Miami.

1980—As unrest grows in Cuba, Castro opens his time-tested escape valve. He allows the disaffected to leave, triggering the Mariel boatlift. Flotillas from Miami go to the Cuban port of Mariel to pick up refugees. Within weeks, 125,000 Cubans make the trip across the Florida Straits and land in Miami. Some 25,000 are criminals and mental patients. The influx severely strains the city's infrastructure. Another test soon arrives: In Tampa, a jury acquits four Miami police officers in the beating death of a black Miamian, Arthur McDuffie. The reaction in Miami is swift and brutal as rioting breaks out in Liberty City. The riots last three days, leaving 18

MILESTONES

dead. Civic leaders go to work to help the black community, but the city seems spiritless. Racial rioting of lesser intensity will repeat itself in 1982, 1984 and 1989 (when the Super Bowl is being played in town).

1981—Another group of refugees is making its presence felt. Haitians escaping the poverty of their home island are migrating to South Florida in rickety boats. Deemed not eligible for political asylum, they are detained in a federal camp on Krome Avenue. Their plight is dramatized to the world when a boat sinks off Palm Beach County and 33 bodies wash ashore. The national news media are paying more and more attention to Miami, most famously in a Time magazine cover story, "Paradise Lost."

1983—A turnaround in Miami's image—a city built on images—is taking shape. Aiding it is an artist named Christo who has what many believe is an absurd scheme to surround several islands in Biscayne Bay with plastic, transforming them into giant pink lily pads. When Christo completes *Surrounded Islands*, doubters are won over.

1984—The hit television series "Miami Vice" debuts, capitalizing on Miami's reputation as the country's major center for the drug trade. It enhances the city's image as an American Casablanca, a place of glamorous danger and intrigue. "Miami Vice" also gives the world a portrait of a city of rich, tropical colors and Deco buildings. On a more prosaic note, Metrorail opens.

PAN AM'S EARLY DAYS: A Pan Am Clipper seaplane docks at Miami's Dinner Key on Biscayne Bay. (Herald file photo)

A new cultural center, designed in a Mediterranean style by architect Philip Johnson, opens. It includes the Center for the Fine Arts, the main public library and the Historical Museum of Southern Florida. Miami has traditionally had an inferiority complex about its perceived lack of culture. The cultural center will help change the perception as will formation of the Miami City Ballet in 1985 and the New World Symphony in 1988. The Miami Book Fair International, organized in 1985, will attract national attention.

1985—Xavier Suarez becomes the first Cuban-American mayor of Miami.

1986—The 47-story CenTrust Tower, designed by architect I.M. Pei, nears completion. For several years, the city's skyline has been reaching higher. South of the Miami River, Brickell Avenue has been undergoing a transformation, too, as condominiums and commercial buildings designed by imaginative young architects redefine the historic street.

1987—Pope John Paul II visits Miami. President Ronald Reagan travels to the city to meet him. Bayside Marketplace opens downtown, becoming the city's primary tourist attraction. One measure of Miami's coming of age and its uniqueness: Within a single year, three books on the city appear in bookstores nationwide.

1988—Joe Robbie Stadium opens. The Miami Heat profes-

MILESTONES

sional basketball team plays its first season.

1990—Dade County's population nears 2 million, approximately half of it of Hispanic origin, including more than a half million Cubans. Although Cuban and Haitian refugees have drawn most of the attention, Miami is a magnet for other immigrants. According to the U.S. Census Bureau, other significant refugee groups include 74,244 Nicaraguans, 68,634 Puerto Ricans, 53,582 Colombians, 23,475 Dominicans, 23,193 Mexicans, 18,102 Hondurans and 16,452 Peruvians.

1991—The airline industry is in the midst of major financial upheaval. Eastern and Pan Am stop flying.

1992—Miami's old nemesis, the hurricane, pays another call, this time in the form of Hurricane Andrew. With highest winds estimated at more than 160 mph, the storm cut a wide path of destruction through South Dade. Storm-related deaths total 38. Damage is estimated at $20 billion. Twenty-five thousand homes are destroyed and 100,000 damaged.

1993—With the first season of the Florida Marlins baseball team, and the Florida Panthers ice hockey team, South Florida will become one of only a handful of urban areas with four professional sports teams.

1994—Thousands of Cubans set out from the island for Miami on flimsy rafts. They are intercepted at sea and interned in camps at the U.S. Navy base at Guantanamo Bay. Meanwhile, the city cements its reputation as the crossroads of the Americas by hosting a summit of 34 heads of government from all over the hemisphere.

1995—As summer approaches, rafters again begin leaving Cuba. With anti-immigration sentiments high throughout the country, President Bill Clinton institutes a new policy on Cuban refugees. The 25,000 Cubans remaining in the Guantanamo camp will be allowed to come to the United States. Rafters will be intercepted and returned to Cuba. After three decades, Cubans are no longer automatically allowed into the United States.

1996—On July 28, Miami is 100 years old.

SEEKING REFUGE: Cuban refugees packed the decks of the *Capt. Preston* as it arrived in Key West in May 1980. They were among thousands who arrived in South Florida during the Mariel Boatlift. (*Herald* file photo)

BOATS, PLANES, TRAINS, AND A TOUCHDOWN

NOW IS THE TIME

HISTORIANS

Arva Moore Parks: [Miami is a] history of arrival. It's really that simple. From the beginning of the founding of the City of Miami, the whole purpose of the city was to try to get people to come down... and seek a new home and seek a new beginning.... The freeze of 1894–95—we've had people who've had terrible things happen in their lives who've come here to start over. There's a great history of that—after World War II people came down and started over.

Howard Kleinberg: Everybody thinks [multiethnicity] is something new. And it's hardly the case because when Miami first arrived as a city in 1896, it already was multiethnic in its way. I think it was Isidor Cohen who wrote that 12 of the first 16 merchants in Miami were Jewish. Half the names on the city charter are those of black people. There was a Cuban cigar maker, Luis Gonzalez, in Miami. There was a Chinese laundry in those first stores. There were Portuguese fishermen who lived in the Grove area... a whole bunch of different people clinging to their beliefs and cultures is the history of Miami of a hundred years. It's not new.

Dr. Paul George: I was also thinking in terms of starting over about all these boomers who came down here in the '20s from other places—in a sense, starting over, hoping to strike it rich.... It was an early Lotto for a lot of people.

Dr. Juan Clark: In the case of the Cubans in particular I might say that Miami was not something new to Cubans. Cubans have been coming to Miami from Cuba as tourists and also as political exiles way back to the '30s. The famous dictator, Machado, came here in exile.... I came here as a tourist back in 19—I don't remember now—in 1950, in 1952 or so. So Miami was not alien, really, to Cuban culture.... Of course when the radical change took place in Cuba with Mr. [Fidel] Castro, then of course it was a natural thing... to come here.

Most actually came as a very temporary place of exile. Gradually

DR. PAUL GEORGE

Dr. Paul George is an associate professor of social history at Miami-Dade Community College, and historian to the Historical Museum of Southern Florida.

DR. JUAN CLARK

Dr. Juan Clark is a professor of sociology at Miami-Dade Community College.

DOROTHY JENKINS FIELDS

Dorothy Jenkins Fields, social studies specialist with Dade County Public Schools, is founder and archivist of the Black Archives in South Florida.

ARVA MOORE PARKS

Historian Arva Moore Parks has written a number of award-winning books and films including Miami: The Magic City.

HOWARD KLEINBERG

Howard Kleinberg, editor of the former Miami News, *is a* Herald *special contributor.*

HISTORIANS

it became home as a result of the events as we know: the Bay of Pigs and the Missile Crisis, etcetera. And gradually roots began to develop.... I have all my children practically born here and my parents buried here, so I definitely call this home now, and I think that's becoming increasingly the case to a large portion of Cubans.

Dorothy Fields: I think part of the myth is that most of the early blacks came from the Bahamas and that was not necessarily the case. There were blacks from the Southern states following the railroad....

And, in the case of Miami, we're talking about the city actually being incorporated the same year in which Plessy vs. Ferguson, landmark Supreme Court case, said that it was all right to be separate but equal, which of course is an oxymoron.

Arva Moore Parks: The whole arrival concept has always fascinated me, mainly because I arrived at Jackson Memorial Hospital as soon as I could [laughter].... Dottie couldn't have been born there, but she was born nearby.... I think that we've always had no more than 10 percent of the people who lived in Miami being native-born.

I've been doing a lot of research on Julia Tuttle and I was just going back and rereading something that her mother had written from here in the 1870s. It said that if you come down here, be prepared to hear every language you can think of....

Julia Tuttle saw us as a great port because there weren't airplanes, obviously, in her day but she saw it as the great city of the southland; the great port, the connector port.

... Henry Flagler had steamships; within a year he had steamships to Nassau and then a year later to Havana. You know, it's always been a dream, it's always been a plan; it's even been reality, particularly with Pan Am.

Dr. Paul George: It's been a city that has reached out to so many people as opposed to, say, an insular city somewhere in Central Florida or Northern Florida.

Howard Kleinberg: The town has no roots. The town *has* roots but nobody will recognize them. Each brings his and her roots from somewhere else and doesn't plant them in our soil, but puts them in a flower pot in the corner of their house and says, "This is my Cleveland . . . and it's always with me." And they still wear their New York Jets football jerseys or their Chicago Blackhawks hockey jerseys....

That's what got me into history. In 1980, we had Mariel and we had the McDuffie [riots] and the town was comin' apart at the seams and nobody had a sense of place anymore. We just seemed to have lost it and we're all—here's the Cubans over there, there's the blacks over there, there's the Anglo rednecks over here, and so on and so forth.... But that is the constant problem of Miami. And I don't think it will ever change.

Nancy Ancrum: Do you run up against that, Dorothy, as a native?

Dorothy Fields: Yes and no. There's so many people out there who, in fact, are very proud of their heritage, that they graduated from Booker T. Washington High School, that they're from Overtown. And I think in a way we have kind of a different feeling about it.

Howard Kleinberg: I think Dorothy would probably, possibly, agree, that the black population of Miami is probably more native to Miami than the white population.

Dorothy Fields: Yes.

Arva Moore Parks: Howard sometimes calls me a sense-of-place person, but I am, because place is our commonality whether we've been here forever or for two weeks.

Sam and Ruth Charin

BY MARILYN ADAMS

They came for a month and stayed forever.

Sam: We came down originally for a month. I had just retired from business. I was 54.

Ruthie wasn't too well and she just couldn't take the northern climate. We were in New Jersey.

Ruth: The doctor suggested either Israel or Florida, because there is no industry that would pollute the air and the climate was so ideal.

Sam: We came down for a month, and it was one of those rare, beautiful Miami winters. It was exceptional.

Ruth: And I suddenly felt like a million dollars....

[Sam] had a brother here. My sister followed me down. She's in Broward. My children lived in South Dade. We had close family. Our children and grandchildren were around us. We were very, very lucky. Sam was young and healthy enough to enjoy his golf. I even played golf here a couple of times.

Sam: We were a group from the beach here who had a car pool and played golf Monday, Wednesday and Friday. [We had] a lot of friends. A lot of them were snowbirds that used to come down [from New Jersey].

Ruth: We still maintained our home up north and still maintained our club up north, so we were socially involved with many of the same people. And it was wonderful.

Sam: We were all a lot younger then.

Ruth: Of course we were—I think the funniest part of Sammy's relationship with his country club was that they had a club within a club—called the Matzoh Balls!

Marilyn Adams

Marilyn Adams is a Herald *product marketing manager and a former reporter.*

BY
ARMANDO SALGUERO

IRVING FRYAR

*A wide receiver for the
Miami Dolphins,
he knows the gospel truth.*

CORNHUSKER FUMBLES

Well, [the University of Nebraska Cornhuskers] had had a great season. We were ranked No. 1 before the season started. At that point we had gone 12-0. We were playing great and we were having fun. Mike Rozier was the Heisman Trophy candidate winner. Turner Gill and myself were also in the running for the Heisman Trophy. We were all All-American going to the bowl games afterward. Our team was doing great. We were a favorite in the game and we felt very confident going in. The game had its ups and downs just like any other game that we played. It came down to the last drive and we managed to get the ball and go down and, of course, the pass where I dropped the touchdown, that was a big play, but managed to be null and void, because a few plays later we managed to score. It came down to whether we were going to go for two points or not, and we went for the two points and we failed. Therefore, we lost the national championship. It was a big disappointment for myself.

Even though it's been over 10 years now, that's something people remember me by. That kind of hurts, because it's just a case with people in general, they seem to remember people for negative stuff, not really positive stuff, and in that realm, it hurts sometimes.

It's not easy. You kind of get a feeling of numbness. You start hating people, not wanting to be around people, not trusting people, watching your back all the time, sheltering yourself, hibernating, and not going out. I went through all of that. I thank God I didn't lose my mind.

HOWEVER...

Miami was the place where I wanted to wind up, because of football. It wasn't so much the place. I didn't know how good the place could be until I got down here. It was the football team, the tradition,

IRVING FRYAR

Don Shula, Dan Marino, the guys I played against twice a year. They seemed to be having fun.

When I came down here, I got on a team that was on the move, that was a passing team, that had confidence in me and that let me go out and play. I just fit right in.

I had things to prove. Not so much to players, but to coaches. I had heard different rumors that coaches didn't want me for one reason or another, because they thought I was a drug addict or a troublemaker.

I had experimented with drugs, but I was not physically addicted to drugs.... It was times when I was depressed that I would use drugs.

So I had something to prove to the coaches across the league. I had something to prove to myself, because people were always talking about this potential that Irving Fryar has. I felt more than anything that I had something to prove to myself. That I could go out and play on the same level as these guys. I always knew that I could, I just needed the opportunity, and I got the opportunity when I came down here.

This is the most important thing that happened to me—or didn't happen to me—since I've been in Miami. When I came down here, they never ever said anything about my past. They never said, "Keep your nose clean." Nothing, nothing ever like that. You don't know what that did for me, for them not to ever mention that. They just gave me the ball and let me run with it. I knew this was the place I needed to be.

THE DIFFERENCE

I was a boy when I came here with the Nebraska Cornhuskers. Between boy and man, confused, wandering in the wilderness and not knowing where I was going or if I was going to get out. A lot of doubt and a lot of fear.

I was a man when I came back down here in 1993 and the difference is the Holy Ghost, the Holy Spirit. It says in the Bible that when Jesus died on the cross that he got the comforter, and that's the Holy Spirit. That's our conscience and that's the man that lives inside of us. When I came down here in 1993 I had that.

It's not that I changed my character, because when I preach it's me that is preaching. It's the outgoing, the vibrant, the loud, the jubilant Irving Fryar that preaches. I don't try to be somebody else. I don't try to preach like somebody else. I jump around and hoot and holler and I make a lot of noise, just like when I'm around the guys.

It's the same Irving Fryar. It's just that I have the Holy Spirit now, which leads me and guides me and tells me yes and tells me no. It makes a big difference and it has made a big difference in my life.

I'm blessed. There's joy, there's peace, there's happiness and all of that that comes with being saved. My family is saved. It just makes me feel good to have a family, because when I was 17 or 18 years old, if you would have said I would have four kids when I was 32, and be playing for the Miami Dolphins and have a couple of businesses and preaching, I would have told you, "You're crazy."

ARMANDO SALGUERO

Herald *sportswriter Armando Salguero covers the Miami Dolphins.*

BY JOHN LANTIGUA

HERBERT KARLINER

A refugee on the ship St. Louis, *he vowed to return if he survived the Holocaust. He did—and he has.*

THE PROMISE

The first time I saw Miami was in the beginning of June 1939. We were on the ship *St. Louis*, and we couldn't reach Havana. We were cruising around in the Straits of Florida, and the captain was closing in near Miami.

We were hoping maybe we could come to the United States.

I cannot tell you exactly what day it was, but all of a sudden we saw Miami, the coast of Miami. I was about 12 years old, and we must have been out of Miami about two miles or so.

We had binoculars and I saw Miami, and I was so impressed with it.

Believe me when I tell you, I said, "Someday I'm going to come back here." What I saw of Miami—it must have been South Beach. I remember there was a little wall, and behind the wall I saw cars driving, and then there [were] the hotels, the white buildings, which was very impressive for us, because in Europe we did not have white buildings like this....

Hopefully we were coming in to Miami; later on I found out the captain was trying to get the boat as close as possible, and if some passenger wanted to jump overboard, he would have let him.

But all of a sudden a Coast Guard cutter came and chased us away from Miami. We were too close.

I saw palm trees, because we never saw palm trees before. This place was something special, and I promised myself that the first time I can make it, I'll come back to Miami.

BEFORE THE VOYAGE

The situation in Germany for Jews was getting worse and worse. My father was taken at Kristalnacht in November 1938 to a concentration camp, to Buchenwald. When he came back we didn't recognize him.... To get him out of the concentration camp we had to prove that we'd leave Germany in the next six months.

We found out that the Cuban consul in Hamburg was selling permits to go to Cuba. So we bought six

HERBERT KARLINER

permits. We were four children and my parents.

We left Germany on May 13, 1939, and we went to Cuba. We had a wonderful trip. The captain and the crew were very nice to us. The food was delicious, we had a lot of fun. It was a cruise ship.

We hoped to get off in Havana, stay there until our quota would be ready to come to the States. Well, when we got to Havana, naturally the Cuban government wouldn't let us in—because of political reasons. The first Spanish word I learned was *mañana*.

We stayed in the port for about a week—five, six days. Finally they say, "You have to move out." The government told us it cost too much money to stay there. So we're cruising around. We're sending telegrams all over the world to let us in—to Panama, to Argentina, to the United States, to no avail.

We sent a telegram to President Roosevelt . . . no answer. Sent a telegram to Mrs. Roosevelt to let the children in, no answer either. So it was very depressing, and we know very well if we go back to Germany what will happen to us.

So we were cruising around and finally we didn't have enough food and water on the ship and the captain gets orders to come back to Europe. You can imagine how the people felt.

Just two days before we arrived [in] Germany, Holland, Belgium, France, and England decided to let us in. Each country took 200 passengers.

I came to France with my family. A few months later, the war broke out, Sept. 3. A year later, the Germans overran France again.

THE PROMISE FULFILLED

I came [to the United States] in 1946, was in Hartford about a year . . . went to night school. There I met another friend. He had been in the concentration camp. His parents were deported, but they had some money here. His cousin gave him other money, so he bought a car. He was a butcher, and we talked. He said, "You know, I would like to go to Florida for the winter."

"Florida!" I said, "When are we going?"

We packed up our things, and we drove down to Miami.

Must have been New Year's 1949. It was like a paradise, I'll always remember that. The flowers, the weather. Hartford was freezing—ice. Here the sunshine and—unbelievable.

In 1953, they built the Fontainebleau hotel. I felt I needed a lot more learning for the bakery, and I went to the Fontainebleau hotel and applied for a job. But all the pastry chef [jobs] were taken because they came out from the Waldorf-Astoria—big guys. I spoke to the chef, and he looked like he likes me and said if you want to work as a helper—.

I said I'll take anything. I went in as a helper at the Fontainebleau Hotel.

I worked there for a few months, and I graduated very fast there. I was made a night chef, and then I was assistant pastry chef. I worked there for 12 years.

Then I left, and I decided to open up my own bakery. I opened up on Biscayne Boulevard and 127th Street, and I called it Michelle's Bakery because my daughter's name is Michelle.

JOHN LANTIGUA

John Lantigua is a Herald *reporter.*

BY
JANE WOOLDRIDGE

June Taylor

*Her dancers—
and Jackie Gleason—
dazzled a nation.*

I was one of the many dancers who had been dancing at the Palmer House in Chicago, and I have to confess I came [to Miami] the first time in 1933. I had just turned 16 years old. However, I passed for 19, which was my object because I wanted to dance. I left school—I graduated from grammar school, but I went three months to high school and wanted to dance. [I] had an opportunity to come here with a group of dancers because we were brought up as lovely dancers who only worked at hotels, no nightclubs.

It was thrilling to get on a Pullman porter train. We had our own beds, and I remember so well the first time we approached warm weather. It was Fort Lauderdale, and I remember looking out the windows and the trainman yelling "Fort Lauderdale, Fort Lauderdale." We looked out the window and all we saw was some palm trees and nothing else.

It was an hour before we arrived in Miami, and we were so excited! The only real thing that I remember so well is going into the train station. We got off the train, and there on my left was the county court building. It was so beautiful, that was really the only building around. Oh, I do remember the [Freedom Tower]. It was pink and white, and it was a beautiful building.

The limousines had picked us up and drove us all the way out. At the time it seemed so far to go from the train station out to Coral Gables, but it was a beautiful area. Lovely little homes, and of course this magnificent Miami Biltmore Hotel. It was pink and white and it was gorgeous!

[We were here] just before New Year's, it was the very end of December, and we spent New Year's Eve and spent the month of January, February, and into March. Then I came back again with three girls, the Merriel Abbott Dancers. We were called the Four Abbotteers. I came back at the end of 1935.

JUNE TAYLOR

In the early '40s, I opened my group in New York with Duke Ellington. That was really my first big step into the big time with the June Taylor Dancers. It was the end of that year that I came back down to Florida in 1945. There was a beautiful, beautiful nightclub on Dade Boulevard, over on the beach called the Copacabana. Kay Thompson and the Four Williams Brothers, Danny Kaye—that was one of his big steps—Sophie Tucker, and the June Taylor Dancers were there for the whole season.

Then across the street was another nightclub called the Beachcomber. It was more money, so I took my June Taylor Dancers over there the following year. In the meantime, I had gotten married to a wonderful man, a theatrical lawyer.

I was down in Florida every year from '45, '46, '47, and '48, four years in a row. Forty-eight is when I started with Ed Sullivan, and then the next time I came to Florida it was 1953 in Miami Beach.

I had about six different groups before I went on television, but when I was doing the nightclubs here in the '40s, I had groups all over the country. I made the rounds, but I still wasn't doing the thing I wanted to do.

I had worked with Jackie [Gleason] in 1946 in Baltimore and I started with him in 1950 on a [television] show called "Cavalcade of Stars" for two years. Then CBS offered him a good contract and I went with him to CBS in 1952 . . . and went on till 1958.

He wanted to go off the air; he had gone as far as he could go and besides he had some movies to do. He went to Paris and did *Gigot*. He came back and did a Broadway show. He did *The Hustler*. He did several movies.

CBS in the early '60s begged him to go back, so the show came back again in 1962. We were in New York in 1962 and 1963, and on the hiatus of the second year we came to Florida because we were all playing golf at that time.

In New York, when it turned cold and the snow came, Jackie could not play golf. When it turned cold, we came down [to] Palm Beach—my husband and I, his manager and his wife, and Jackie, who wasn't married at the time.

We were having dinner at Petite Marmite and I was sitting opposite Jackie. I had just put the spoon in my soup and he said, "I think we should come down to Florida and do the show here. We can play golf."

I just stopped and said, "Do the show down here? I don't think I could work down here, Jackie."

"Why?" he said. I said, "Well, because it's vacationland. I have to have New York where there's inspiration and a different ballgame. This is vacationland, I don't think I could work here. I couldn't rehearse here with the sun shining."

He said that what we should do was rehearse at night and pull the shades down and pretend you are in New York. At any rate, he wanted to come down and I didn't think I could come and he said to try it.

So he got me there and I had to try it. So we came down, and it was working. I found I could do not only the shows, but much more because I was outdoors with the sun and the air.

It added years to my life.

JANE WOOLDRIDGE

Jane Wooldridge is executive editor/producer of Destinations Florida.

ELLY CHOVEL

BY LIZ BALMASEDA

After Castro's rise to power, Elly Chovel was one of 14,000 Cuban children brought—without their parents—to the United States during the Pedro Pan flights.

FIRST GLIMPSE OF MIAMI

I arrived here on the second of June of 1962. No one ever forgets the day that they arrive. It becomes part of your life as if it was your birthday. No one forgets that. And I was 14 years old.

I remember looking out the plane through the little window, and I was looking for the little hills or to see if I saw any rivers, and all I saw was flatness and canals and a beautiful blue sea that was just on the other side of the Straits of Florida—and no mountains. A few royal palms luckily, because that made me feel that it was something not so foreign. But the thing that struck me the most was that it was totally flat, totally flat.

Half of the 14,000 children were picked up by either relatives or designated friends, close friends of the family. But the other half went to the camps that Father [Bryan] Walsh had to accommodate all these thousands of children.

At the beginning, it was only going to be 200 children that he was going to take care of. At the time, he was only a 30-year-old Irish priest.... Little did he know that we were going to multiply like fish.

I was in [Florida City] with my sister for three and a half months. We got there in June, and we finally left about the end of August, the beginning of September, to a foster home.

It was an unbelievable living experience. We were in a camp in Florida City that, at the time the monsignor got it, were apartments that were empty. He made a deal with the mayor of Florida City who had built them, and they fenced them, they built a cafeteria, and in every little apartment lived a couple of Cuban extraction because Father Walsh felt that we would feel better if at least the people that were taking care of us were familiar with us, spoke the same language, and understood where we were coming from.

I lived with a family, Dr. Velasco, who was a dentist, and his wife, and we must have been, I think,

ELLY CHOVEL

around 25 children divided into two very small bedrooms. We had bunk beds. I had never slept on a bunk bed. I shared a bedroom with my sister and that was it. And all of a sudden there were 14 others in the room.

I remember eating Fritos. Fritos were delicious. The coffee—we almost died the first time that we drank the washed-out coffee.

But, it was like a cocoon, it was a cocoon.

GROWING UP

I did fall in love with an Irish boy that I met who had just graduated from college. He was a CPA, and he was in ROTC.

He became an officer. After my parents came from Spain—they had to leave Cuba, go to Spain—and they got to Buffalo, they were there less than a year. They couldn't tolerate the coldness. So they decided to leave.

At this time we came back to Miami.

I then became a stewardess. I was 20. I wanted to be able to have the convenience of flying and being able to see my fiancé. He was being transferred from base to base to get basic training. After he got his commission as a lieutenant, we were married in Miami, right here in Coconut Grove. Had an apartment here.

Then we parted—we went by car, little Mustang, looking at the beautiful United States. We went up the coast of California to Tacoma, Wash., where he went to his second flight school. Then I had a child, my first daughter Brigid, Brigid Antonia.

When she was 5 months, Tom had to leave for Vietnam. We came back to Miami. We bid our good-byes to all of our relatives and friends. It's like he had a foreboding, and he wanted to see each person that we knew was close to us. So we took a little trip and we said good-bye to everyone. I stayed in Miami with Brigid until he was killed. Exactly a week after he died she was 1 year old.

BECOMING AN AMERICAN

[Tom] was all of 23. It was very ironic, because Tom loved his country. I learned to love his country through him, and he was very proud to wear the uniform and represent his country.

Yet he knew that [the war] was a mistake, and once he was there, he wrote me a letter which I got the week that he died. He said how ironic that he will be risking his life for a place so far away from home to save them from communism, when it could have been a lot more understandable if he was risking his life and if he lost it, that at least he could give me back my country.

It was so poetic. So it was very difficult for me to see him offer his life—or waste his life—for something that really made no sense. But there are a lot of things that make no sense.

I became a citizen of the United States because of his death. For some reason, because I became a widow, once you are the widow of a veteran, that gives you special privileges, and I became an American. I always thought that there was something beautiful about this country that everybody came here seeking the same thing—liberty and freedom.

LIZ BALMASEDA

Liz Balmaseda is a Herald *columnist.*

BY
AL TOPPING

NGUYEN VAN LUC

Nguyen Van Luc and three of his daughters emigrated to the United States from Vietnam in 1992. When South Vietnam fell in 1975, he chose to stay with his ailing mother. He now works for United Airlines.

In Vietnam I only knew about Miami city as I watched on TV. Also in some pictures on the newspapers. I like to be there, and I expect to learn a lot of things about the new life. Not only for me, but for my children too.

One time I saw some pictures on the newspaper. Some pictures of Miami city and the living of the Cubans. I remember that most of the pictures were nice pictures. Beautiful pictures, beautiful city.

I remember my country because of the weather here. The weather here is the same one like in Vietnam. Some of the fruits and plants are the same ones like in Vietnam.

In every city or country you have nice people and not-so-nice people. It is the same in Vietnam.

The most I like is there is no difficulties with the local authorities. I am very moved by the full assistance by people. I never knew them before. I never meet them before.

The driving is the same situation in Vietnam. Sometimes we meet bad drivers and sometimes we meet very nice drivers. They know how to drive and to keep the traffic flowing. That is the same case in Vietnam.

AL TOPPING

Al Topping is assistant manager for the Herald's *pressroom operations. He was operations manager in Vietnam for Pan American Airlines until 1975. Mr. Nguyen, his colleague, was ramp operations manager at that time. Mr. Topping arranged the last flight out, ferrying 463 Vietnamese employees. It took him 17 years—and miles of red tape—to engineer Mr. Nguyen's departure.*

BUGS, BIRDS, BOUGAINVILLEA— AND A SWAMP

THE NATURE OF THIS PLACE

HISTORIANS

Arva Moore Parks: Until about 1947 . . . the prevailing opinion was the Everglades existed to be drained. Even though there were those that, you know, were speaking otherwise. . . . Some of the great naturalists, like [John] Gifford, wrote books on draining the Everglades. . . . The *Miami Herald* actually ran a contest to change the name of the Everglades because it was full of snakes and alligators, and the winning person renamed the Everglades "The Prairie Garden."

We now know, thanks to Marjory [Stoneman Douglas] and others, that we need the Everglades for our water supply, not just because of birds and snakes. . . . When the governors of Florida . . . began the drainage, that was like the biggest, most wonderful thing that had ever happened to this state.

Howard Kleinberg: And at the time [the Australian pine, the melaleuca, and the Brazilian pepper] were introduced, they thought they were good.

Dr. Paul George: Our problem, up until '47 at least, was too much water. Now, of course, we have these droughts. . . . All the hoopla about draining the 'Glades or digging these drainage ditches; the creation of the South Florida Water Management District; all this stuff is just marvelous, high-tech-type stuff. Now we regret a lot of this.

Howard Kleinberg: But we have this one wonderful constant and that's called the Palmetto bug. . . .

Even going back to the Spanish, [they were] complaining about the mosquitoes in Miami. . . . I'm going to write the great Miami mosquito book someday.

Dr. Paul George: I'm dealing in South Dade history now. And I can't emphasize enough how much mosquitoes come up in the average discourse.

Arva Moore Parks: That's where I become an old-timer because I remember when the mosquitoes were awful. You didn't even go to Coconut Grove in the summer time 'cause you couldn't get through it without being eaten alive. . . . A million people in Miami today live on former wetlands. The Everglades started on 27th Avenue.

Nancy Ancrum: Talk about heat.

Dr. Paul George: Everybody headed to North Carolina in the summers.

Howard Kleinberg: Now wait. If you go back and look at all these great photos of our pioneers [in the late 1800s]; they're all walking around downtown Miami with starched, stiff collars, ties, jackets, and hats. Nobody passed out. . . .

Everything is relative . . . we didn't have air-conditioned schools, right? The windows were open. They built them that way. There were breezeways. I don't remember perspiring that much when I went to school.

Dorothy Fields: It's called sweating.

Arva Moore Parks: But another

HISTORIANS

thing about nature that you didn't mention besides catching the breeze is, "Don't live beneath the ridge." The great Atlantic coastal ridge that goes right down South Florida.

Nancy Ancrum: Sunlight.

Howard Kleinberg: You used the word "heat"; it's not really the heat, it's the humidity.

Dr. Paul George: Sunlight's interesting. It drew people down for reasons of health, for reasons of beauty, comfort, and now, of course, it's a no-no to get too much of it.

Howard Kleinberg: There's one interesting thing that newcomers probably could not believe in Miami. I know when I was going to high school . . . in the mornings when you get into your shoes, you looked first and shook them first to see if there were scorpions in them.

Nancy Ancrum: When I moved down here I found the most intriguing thing besides the quality of the sunlight—the rain. . . .

Howard Kleinberg: I always say on those rare days when it's solid overcast all day, I say it's like a day in Pittsburgh; it's not a Miami day. A Miami day is where you get [rain] about 4 o'clock, well actually about 7 in the morning coming in from the coast. . . . And then 4 in the afternoon coming in from the Everglades, you get these good, you know, 20-minute gully washers. I have no problem with them; they're delightful.

Arva Moore Parks: I love our rain. Our kind of rain. I use this as a metaphor for Miami so many times and I always tell the story, particularly about storm and sunshine. . . . It sums us up. . . . About every afternoon about 20 after 3, like Howard just said, this enormous black cloud appears over the Everglades, a black menacing cloud that roars across town, and it just rains like the dickens and it blows over and the sun comes back out. . . . We are a green world.

Howard Kleinberg: I never fail to marvel when I get off a plane coming from somewhere in the United States or somewhere, other than Latin America, and that humidity smacks you in the face. I, for one, love it. You know you're in Miami.

Dr. Juan Clark: And the green is something that really . . . when you fly in wintertime anywhere, everything is, you know, dark or whatever, burned. And back to Miami, the green all the time there, the grass is really an exhilarating experience, I think. So that's why I say I would never live anywhere else.

Arva Moore Parks: And there's something about weather in the tropics and subtropics and I think you can use that, again as almost a metaphor, for all the rapid change. We grow things so fast.

Howard Kleinberg: Did you ever try to get rid of a banana tree? Cannot be done. Or a bamboo. Cannot be done.

BY MARTHA MUSGROVE

JANET RENO

Janet Reno is attorney general of the United States.

CLEVER TONY

In 1943, I was 5. We had a brown-and-white blue-eyed pony named Tony, [another named] Dottie, and two donkeys, Felix and Pedro. Some animals are smarter than others.

Dottie, the brown pony, was shrewd and calculating. Tony was shrewd, but he loved oats. You could shake a pan of oats at him and eventually he'd give in. His stomach was bigger than his laziness. He always pulled the buggy. He could pull four kids, my mother, and father in the buggy.

My mother learned how to shoe horses. I held a leg.

I learned horse etiquette by experience. Tony would take me up to a [tree] branch and slowly walk under it [trying to knock me off]. Mother stood there and said, "He's going to do that until you show him who's boss."

SPARKS FLY

There were some lime trees on our land but mostly it was scrub, [just pine and palmetto] that had been timbered. So you could see stumps. It had been used as a farm. There was an old cattle chute—just pine and palmetto. The Seaboard Railroad track was about two miles down the road. Now and then a spark would fly off and set a fire on the glade.

Nothing stood between us and the glade [although] we had firebreaks, and I remember lighting backfires.

My mother and father . . . always got us into the spirit of things. I can remember they gave us a sense of security. I don't remember being afraid. I remember being in awe of the fire. I remember them telling us that we were going to have to help them. I didn't understand how backfires worked, but I trusted my Mom and I remember thinking, "Gee, they work."

STARGAZING

I had bought a 60-power reflecting telescope.

JANET RENO

I ordered it from *Sky and Telescope* magazine. Mother was wonderful about telling us which star was which. Miami was a small town then, and you weren't disturbed by the lights of the city. The stars were crystal clear and the trees had not grown up. I remember the day I found the moons of Saturn. I was about 12 or 13. I hadn't had it very long. Saturn hadn't been visible. It was unmistakable. The telescope was incredible.

Martha Musgrove

Martha Musgrove is an associate editor of the Herald.

BY ARNOLD MARKOWITZ

GILBERT CLARK

Gilbert Burleson Clark retired in 1989 as senior forecaster of the National Hurricane Center. If ever offered a choice between heaven and hell, he is likely to hesitate. "Gosh," he'll say, "I'm not sure. Can I see the weather reports?"

FIRST, LAST FLIGHT OUT

The first [hurricane] flight I was on was with a university professor from Florida State. He and I were on this plane with a group. They had a colonel and a bunch of military people on board. We flew from the Cape down to San Juan and then we flew into Hurricane Connie, August 1955.

So we flew into Connie about 1,000 miles east of San Juan, and we had some real wild experiences. Nobody on the plane had ever been in a hurricane. We didn't know anything about anything and this old B-29 wasn't exactly in good shape. It was a World War II plane.

They put this professor up in the nose as a navigator to get us into the eye, and he was reading the instruments wrong and this equipment luckily had an automatic cutoff at 500 feet so bells would start ringing, telling you that your automatic navigation equipment wasn't working as you were below 500 feet.

We were supposed to be at 2,000 feet flying into the storm and all of a sudden the bells start ringing and they find out this professor was reading the [atmospheric] pressure backwards. . . . We were going right into the water if it hadn't been for that automatic navigational equipment on board with the bells. The colonel cusses, "Get this son-of-a-bitch out of the nose and put the regular captain in there."

The plane lost an engine in the eye. Then the second engine on the same flight started losing oil pressure, and they called the Coast Guard. When I got back to San Juan, I got out and kissed the ground. I thought we were dead. The crew were all shook up. What a mess to get into. . . . I [said] "This may be fun flying into hurricanes, but I'd rather be forecasting them than fly in them." So I came [to Miami] in August 1955 as a research forecaster and I have been here ever since.

We had a big staff. A 10-man office, which is

GILBERT CLARK

pretty good for what they had before. We were in Lindsey Hopkins, top floor. We stayed there until the new radar came. In 1958 they brought a new radar. They couldn't put it on top of the Lindsey Hopkins; it was too big. So we moved to the Aviation Building where National Airlines had this building on 36th Street and 27th Avenue.

We moved into the fifth floor, and the Navy moved into the fourth floor. So with the Navy and us, we coordinated back and forth. The Navy helped coordinate advisories during that period—in the late '50s until 1964. In 1964 we still weren't called hurricane forecasters or hurricane specialists. We were still writing the state forecast, the local forecast and writing advisories.

When I first came here in 1955 all we had were a few ship reports and we had a Navy and Air Force that would fly into a storm—if we knew where it was. We didn't know where any storms were. We didn't have any satellites. So we had no idea of knowing where a storm was until a ship wandered into it.

Then finally about 1958 or 1959 they decided to fly an Air Force plane that would take off from Puerto Rico and make a long triangular flight over the Atlantic for a thousand miles. It was a 12-hour flight and they would look for the weather. They were just searching. They didn't know what they were seeing because they always kept reporting this haze. We didn't know it was African dust that they were seeing. It was haze technically, but it came from the African dust. Anyway, they flew out and made these long trips. Occasionally they would find a storm. We didn't have a real radar system when I first came here. We had a little miniature airplane radar that was used here at the Miami office to watch storms. It was on the roof of the Lindsey Hopkins. It was very small radar. We had a 75-mile range on it. We had no radar anywhere else.

In the early '60s the satellite became more and more operational. By 1963 or 1964 we had pictures of the whole area and we could actually make loops where you could see the motion of the clouds and see the circulation come off of Africa.

Satellites haven't really changed a whole lot except that we've got better satellites up there that see better pictures. We can take pictures every 15 minutes.

Also this new satellite that they have up now, it can give us some idea what kind of atmosphere we have in the tropics even when there are no clouds. They will be able to see when there are cold pockets of air or warm pockets of air in the atmosphere based on the sounding from this big satellite. And we can also pick up the wind. They now have a computer that can take the cloud motion and make big maps showing the circulation all around the globe. Now we actually see the wind as it really is based on the satellite loops.

ARNOLD MARKOWITZ

Arnold Markowitz is a Herald *reporter.*

BY
RICHARD WALLACE

MORT COOPER

Mort Cooper has some fine-feathered friends. His only regret is that there are not as many as there used to be.

I came down here [in February 1954] basically to enjoy the birding and the fishing all year round, which I could not do in Pennsylvania. I worked for an engineering firm as a graphic illustrator; worked on the Bob Tail Turnpike, as the Florida turnpike... was known as then.

When you got as far west as where 117th Avenue is now, you were in the Glades. There were no salt dams on the canals, so there were snook and tarpon in the canals along with freshwater bass. There were Indians living east of where 177th Avenue is now. Miccosukees had chickees east of 117th on the south side of Bird Road.

And when I first came down I was fishing an awful lot. I would go out on the Bird Road Canal. Beyond 117th [there] was just a little dirt road out there and you could stop and fish the spots along the canal, and there's nothing like seeing a 30-pound tarpon come shimmering up in full moonlight—catching the moonlight up out of the canal after you have been fighting him for half an hour. It's just a beautiful sight.

I probably had a fishing rod in my hand as much as I did binoculars, but I never went anywhere without both, so I was always watching. Any time I was fishing I was still watching birds.

I slowly became more of a—not an environmentalist—more of a preservationist.... I really believe in wilderness areas. I believe people should stay out of them. There should be sanctuaries... that we don't have to get into, because when man gets into something, into a place at any wilderness area, he's disturbing whatever's there even if it doesn't look like it.

I slowly took a lot of the birding walks and different things that were going on with Audubon, particularly, and used to go down to the Tortugas.... We used to go down there for 70 bucks for a weekend. Of course it's seven times that [now]. So we got more and more involved and when

MORT COOPER

the time came, they asked me to start leading some of the trips.

THESE BIRDS HAVE FLOWN

I don't think there's 10 percent of the birds now that we had back in the '50s. Literally, and maybe a lot of cases 5 percent. When the warbler migration came through, when the redstarts came through in August, you'd see flocks of them and they'd be all over the place.... Black-throated blue warblers: You'd go out and you'd see 200 in a day. You're lucky to see 10 in any one day, even at the height of migration now. So there's just numbers of [birds] completely gone.

We used to drive to Flamingo [in the Everglades], down the old road along the Homestead Canal. ... There was just a fishing village; it hadn't been developed as a visitor center or anything like that by the park yet. And it was just a little dirt road and you had trouble passing somebody if they were going the other way. There were birds all the way down. There were snakes all the way down. Turtles. There were —but the bird life; it was just amazing. There were just flocks and flocks [of] birds. Barred owls would come out in broad daylight to hit a snake on the road. They didn't wait for nightfall.

There used to be rookeries, especially near Flamingo, that was off-limits to boaters and canoers for two, three months a year while the birds were there, nesting. But they roosted down there. Thousands of birds on these two little double islands that turned white every night, every evening, with the bird life, and the birds were that way all the way down.

FLOCK OF BIRD LOVERS

I advertised for some time in *Bird Watchers Digest* and that got people—general birders more than it did specific birders. But the ABA people, American Birding Association people, are more serious birders and they're looking for specific birds they've never seen from our area that wouldn't be anywhere else.... The birds that really excite them are birds that show up accidentally here, lose their way and end up over here in South Florida from the islands and not considered exotic; they're considered accidental like the Greater Antillean peewee that was here last week up at Boca Raton.

People flew in from all over the country.... Well, birders are strange people, too, don't forget, and I mean the last day we went up there, last Saturday, there was a guy [who] flew in from California just to see the bird and there were three guys [who] drove down from Pennsylvania, straight down ... overnight, to see the bird and the bird wasn't there. So they had to return home empty-handed, with their expenditures and their time spent.

You always let it be known that you can't be held responsible for a bird because birds have wings and ... if you promise a bird to somebody—"Hey, I got this one pinned down. I'll show it, I can take you there and guarantee that bird"— that's the day that bird's gonna change his pattern of behavior and not show. It happens all the time.

SQUAWK!!

The parrots date back to the early '70s, a lot of them. And I used to see flocks of red-crowned parrots fly by in South Miami over 20 years ago, 25 years ago, heading for the roost they still use in South Miami. They used to fly by, squawking in the sunset at dusk; they usually go to their roost about sunset. Some usually show up early sometimes, but some nights they don't come in until it's too dark to see them, so these do date back to probably escapees that escaped in the late '60s and started breeding and building up. Different species

MORT COOPER

added to them; there's probably seven species that go to the roosts here in South Florida. Seven Amazon species and occasionally other birds join them. There has been a Senegal parrot lately.

Often these birds are held in quarantine when they're brought into the country from wherever their origin, country of origin was, and they've been known to escape or have been released or accidentally or otherwise from Customs, from quarantine, sometimes from the pet dealers themselves. And enough of them have escaped that they've got together, a lot of them, and parrots are noisy when they fly and any recently escaped parrot will join a flock of other parrots going by and they're very sociable birds that way. And so they feed in flocks, quietly, but when they fly, you usually hear them coming.

Before Hurricane Andrew, where we had large, fairly large areas of casuarina or Australian pine—the taller trees the better; they like to get up high away from predators, including man—and the roosts sometimes had up to 350, 400 birds or more and now, probably lucky to see 150 because they go to several different roosts now.

There may have been some losses. It doesn't seem like there's any species completely wiped out.

It's amazing how birds can survive something as strong as that storm. But they get down behind things. There seemed to be a decrease in native species for a while in what we call ground zero area, where the eye of the storm came across. Birds that are successfully hidden during the first half of the hurricane passing through were caught unawares when the second half came from the opposite side. And they could have gotten blown right out of their hiding places and there were a lot of places where flocks of blackbirds were blown out of grassy areas right into fences and killed against fences. Nesting ibises and herons were blown out of the mangroves. Hundreds and hundreds were killed down there, all along the bayfront in that area.

RICHARD WALLACE

Richard Wallace is an editor on the Herald's *national desk.*

By Nancy Ancrum

Dina Knapp

Dina Knapp, of Miami Beach, finds art in the flora and fauna of South Florida, then encases it in vinyl—bugs included.

I started collecting all those kitschy things, like when you go to Woolworth's.... It was just so indicative of this place. It's hard to pass the Shell Man.... there are lots of Shell Men on the roads as you come down from South of the Border, which I love. I love that drive.

There's all those ticky-tacky places, and they sell the dolphins—the plastic—and the shells. I started collecting all that stuff not really knowing what was going to happen, and it all somehow got focused.

I started to use postcards, usually postcards of Florida of long ago. When you look at them it's almost like you can close your eyes and make believe you're there and feel what it was like to be in a fancy car and to open the door and walk out onto Ocean Drive into a fancy Art Deco hotel and hear that '30s music and dance.

ART'S PROCESS

Initially I used real plants. I use real bugs. I have some that have totally disintegrated. When you encase them in vinyl, I kind of thought that they would survive. It takes quite a few years, but they turn into a powder.... I used dried fish in one piece. Didn't work.

I realized that the real things aren't going to make it into posterity, so I started buying the fake stuff: fake ants, fake bugs, fake snakes, fake all sorts of creepy crawly things. I'll buy a lot of silk leaves, the palm fronds and fan palms, and use them in the collages.

I think that what happens is that somehow ... a complete statement happens.

Nancy Ancrum

Nancy Ancrum is a member of the Herald's *Editorial Board.*

Capt. Bob Lewis

BY ARNOLD MARKOWITZ

Charter boat captain Bob Lewis has seen a few wrecks in his day— the best places yet to catch fish.

THE FISH WERE BITING

My first guide job was up Tavernier Creek [in the Keys]. There wasn't anything on the creek then, not a house or nothing. Just all mangroves, and if you wanted to catch shrimp you had to catch 'em yourself at night, and the mosquitoes would eat you up, but you had to. Then you'd build a smudge pot.

We had a little five-horsepower Johnson I could use once in a while.

I was about 14, 15, and my anglers would cast, with a plug cast up in the mangroves, and just every cast you'd catch big mangrove snappers. I mean two-, three-, four-, five-pound mangrove snappers.

But of course those are all houses these days. It's just traffic in Tavernier, just like it is here at Government Cut, and worse up in Port Everglades. On a weekend, you can hardly get a boat through there without taking your life in your hands.

Then of course I grew up, and then we fished out of Miami. I went fishing with one of the best fishermen I've ever been out with in my life. Of course he was a commercial fisherman named Andy Schuberth, he had Schuberth's Seafood Restaurant down on the Flagler Street Bridge, and he managed Cap'n Tom's Fishhouse.

We'd go out front, catch Warsaw groupers in handlines and eight-pound sashweights—right out in front of Miami. We'd have different spots out there in 245, 250 feet, and we'd catch double-headers. His boat was grooved down all on the side where you'd have to groove the line down, and it's burned into the wood. But these fish would average over 100 pounds apiece, then you'd bring up maybe two fish 140, 150 pounds a piece.

In four or five hours we could catch six or eight of these big fish, plus red snapper. There was a lot of red snapper out front in those days, big snappers like from 20, 25 pounds. If we got two cents a pound for the groupers, that was

CAPT. BOB LEWIS

good. Sometimes, you couldn't even sell them.

Now if you have them, they're worth a gold mine. But there's no more of them left, there's no more of them left.

GOING PRO

I went on Pier 5 [in Bayfront Park] in 1948, running my own boat. I bought a boat. I was on the police department, that was my first job after the war because you couldn't get jobs. So I took the test and I made the Police Department.

I bought a boat for $1,200—an old landing craft surplus—and I took it up to Norseman Boatyard. They put on a false bow for me for about another $1,200, and my dad helped me and I put a bridge on it. That was my first charter boat, called the Lazy Lady. I got into Pier 5. There were 37 boats up there in those days.

I had 12, 15 wrecks and drops right off of Miami. You'd find them or you'd set up your own wrecks, which was against the law in those days. But we'd sneak one out, like a barge—hell, 2 o'clock in the morning—two of us get together, and we'd put cement in it and we'd go out and sink it.

That's great, because it would attract fish. Nobody else knew where it was. And you'd know the depth of water you're in, that's all you had to know, because you'd take bearings on land. Like one finger or two fingers between the courthouse and pine tree over here. You could catch the same fish that you lost yesterday—very accurate.

Nobody knew where it was, and you wouldn't hit it too hard. If you had a slow day for your people, you'd go in there and get them a couple amberjacks and then you'd leave it. You wouldn't go back the next day and just fish it out. You'd have your different spots to fish.

SWISHING WINGS

The birds—this was back when I was 15, 16, 17, even after the war—we'd go duck hunting. We had Model As, and we'd go across the flats. We'd leave Flamingo and liable to get stuck for a day and a half out there on the flats. Sometimes you'd just be spinning. You didn't dare stop but you'd go down in the muck.

You'd take your own wood to build little bridges, you know—two-foot-tens, to get across the canal.

I've seen the pelicans, white pelicans, in November. They start circling in that area, East Cape. The first day you'd see five or six hundred birds. You could hear 'em with the wings swishing as they come around.

Next day there'd be 1,500, and the next day there'd be 2,000. Then the sky'd be white with them, and all of a sudden they'd all land. The Everglades looked like it'd been snowed on, white Everglades.

And the ducks were the same way, and all the birds, all of the waterbirds, wading birds and so forth.

Then . . . they started to correct nature, and they started to dam everything, and they'd work the water here and they'd work the water there. They thought this was the thing to do, and drain the water in the 'Glades, and that's the end of it. It's not like that anymore, and I doubt if they'll ever get it back to its natural state.

ARNOLD MARKOWITZ

Arnold Markowitz is a Herald reporter.

PIONEERS AND BRICKLAYERS

LAYING MIAMI'S FOUNDATIONS

HISTORIANS

Dorothy Fields: Those [blacks] who came from Southern states came to help build a new city. It's interesting when you look at the original [Miami] charter and you see the names of the men—and they were all men because women could not vote, of course. . . .

But all of the names are written in one hand so it must have been the clerk of the court at the time, and the race is next to it so you know who they are. Most of them, as we've gone through the list, seem to be from the Southern states. There were some few from the Bahamas. . . . We know that a number of the men were very involved with churches because they, in fact, were the organizers for Greater Bethel A.M.E. Church or Mount Zion [Baptist Church] and St. Agnes [Episcopal Church]. Their names appear on those rolls and so they came as artisans, they came as skilled laborers who did what needed to be done in order to help this city.

Arva Moore Parks: We have the pictures of that first group. I think that's very special about this city. The picture of the beginning of the first spade of dirt to clear the side of the Royal Palm [Hotel]. . . . And I tell people that that's like having a picture of a baby in the nursery. What other major city has their foundings so beautifully documented? I love that picture.

Howard Kleinberg: Isidor Cohen [in an article about Miami's incorporation] said that the best speech was made by a "darkie" named Lightbourn. We don't know anything of what Lightbourn said but it's interesting that a white person would acknowledge that the best speech for incorporation was delivered by a black.

Dr. Paul George: I'm just so struck by the fact that for thousands of years—with the exceptions of hurricanes and other natural calamities and a little bit of building on both banks of the Miami River—there was really very little done to alter the environment in any significant way. Yet here we have, in a matter of a couple months, more change physically than we had in the previous—probably with the exception of hurricanes—10,000 years.

Nancy Ancrum: What are those months you're talking about?

Dr. Paul George: Well, we're talking about beginning in early, probably in March of 1896, all the way through, say, incorporation on July 28. This instant city. I've got somewhere, I think it appeared in Arva's book, a photograph of this family that sort of set up shop, circa early 1890s, in the middle of these woods. . . . Contrast that with 1896. It's overwhelming. Here they are clearing this land for the Royal Palm Hotel.

Arva Moore Parks: . . . Within the first three years at least they were calling themselves officially the Magic City. . . . Of course, it wasn't much of a city. It looked like a frontier town.

Dr. Paul George: Then this hotel, though. It's a novelty over there. . . . John D. Rockefeller,

HISTORIANS

Andrew Carnegie, and this little frontier city.

Howard Kleinberg: Painted canary yellow, by the way.

Arva Moore Parks: With a red roof. I mean, think of it. A red roof with a bright yellow building. But that again goes back to the thing that makes me sad about my town. I don't get sad too often. We tore that down in 1930.

Dr. Paul George: [We haven't discussed] the farming/homesteading nature of this area.... But prior to the railroad, the folks who came here came primarily because of the lure of homesteads. And they were all over the place.

Arva Moore Parks: Coconut Grove.... You could still homestead in Homestead into the 20th century. That's an amazing thought for this city that we live in, too. That you could still basically get free land right here in Greater Miami into the 20th century.

Dr. Paul George: In reading these little stories about South Dade, how there was a nine-mile pathway between Silver Palm and Cutler, where the mail was and where the boat came. Yeah, this is 1905 or something, 1910. Again, it speaks for the youth of this last page in Miami's history, the last chapter in this history. Philadelphia was an old city by then.

Howard Kleinberg: You stood on what is now Miami Beach in 1900 and there were only, that I know of, two buildings. One was the House of Refuge on 16th and the other was the Charles Lum house. There were only two buildings there in 1900. Look at it now. It's wall to wall.

Arva Moore Parks: They were building houses of refuge down here because it was so isolated ... to help people who were shipwrecked. And that was built in 1876, so we're very late. I always say it's fun to talk about. Would you want me to talk about how we're one of the oldest habitation sites?... Or do you want me to talk about the youngest major American city? So this dichotomy, I think, has always been part of our history, too. You know, we're just like paradise or we're hell. We're storm or we're sunshine.

Dr. Paul George: Early '80s, it was hellish. The whole "paradise lost" thing and soon after tourism perked up again and the economy got much better, period.

Arva Moore Parks: Let's talk about women. We haven't mentioned women except for Julia [Tuttle].... I made a list of pioneering women; kind of the first this, first that, first this, first that. I had Eleanor Galt Simmons, who was an early doctor, first woman doctor in the Grove, and I made a list of the first architect and the first person on the Commission and the first person here and there and then I ended with every single person on the list that I had listed I had known personally except Eleanor Galt Simmons.... Which, to me, is just an amazing story in itself. Talk about the youngness of this city and the short period in which women have played their proper role in society.

INTERVIEW AND COMPILATION BY GEOFFREY TOMB

MARJORY STONEMAN DOUGLAS

If you've heard of the Everglades, thank this woman.

The year was 1890. Benjamin Harrison was president, a future president—Dwight Eisenhower—was born, the British Empire was ruled by Queen Victoria, 300 Sioux were slaughtered by the U.S. Cavalry at Wounded Knee, S.D., and in Minneapolis, on April 7, Marjory Stoneman gulped her first breath.

During the next century, no human would equal her as both witness and participant in a stunning transformation at the southern tip of the Florida Peninsula. Her handprint is part of an entire culture.

Raised a patrician in New England and a graduate of Wellesley College (Class of 1912), she came to Miami in 1915, after a brief, unhappy marriage, to get a divorce.

She found a city—six years younger than she—at the edge of the subtropical frontier with a population of fewer than 5,000 people.

Eighty years later, she continues to live quietly, tenaciously at her shake-shingle cottage in Coconut Grove, which she built in 1925. In those eight decades, she has turned a swamp into a national cause, marched for women's suffrage, and most important, written with eloquence and passion about the community she made home.

Marjory Stoneman Douglas, in her own words:

"The moonlight on the unpaved streets was like snow."

—*Recollections from December 1915, as she stepped from the train from New York and arrived, for good, in Miami*

"Father, I've just joined the Navy. What's going to happen to the* Herald*?"

Her father, Frank B. Stoneman, was editor of the *Miami Herald* where she was a reporter.

His reply:

"What I'm wondering is what's going to happen to the Navy."

—*Recollections from 1917 (She was honorably discharged to accept a job in*

MARJORY STONEMAN DOUGLAS

the publicity department of the American Red Cross in Europe during World War I.)

"In this city we have the sorriest, most spineless, narrow-minded, nearsighted, pusillanimous lot of so-called civic-minded people of any city on earth. There is but one reason why Miami ever grew past the fish-and-wampum era—God! This place has divine blessing and grows in spite of those stupid, asinine fugitives from a vacuum."

—*Interview with* Miami Herald *columnist Jack Bell, March 1947*

"There is no other Everglades in the world."

—*Opening line in* The Everglades: River of Grass, *1947*

"Yet the springs of fine water had flowed again. The balance still existed between the forces of life and of death. There is a balance in man also, one which has set against his greed and his inertia and his foolishness; his courage, his will, his ability slowly and painfully to learn, and to work together."

—*From ending of the same book*

"I love to be a freelance writer. With no dependents, a well-oiled typewriter, and decent health you can live indefinitely, so to speak, on your own fat.

"Florida is ideal. There are no clothes problem down here. You can wear practically anything you want and get away with it. As for people, those who aren't already here are sure to come sooner or later so you can keep up with all your friends."

—Miami Herald *interview, 1953*

"The thoughtful citizen is aware that evils exist, which, if not checked, will threaten the whole promise of this area.

"One of the gravest problems with which we are faced is the menace of substandard housing and deteriorating, unwholesome neighborhoods. These blighted sections are like a cancerous growth that cannot be contained."

—*Speech to Miami Housing Authority, May 1958*

"Everybody said Paris will be so changed. I had not seen it for 40 years. I found it magnificent and utterly familiar. It is the same Paris that I knew well. After 40 years, a war and a lot of depression, it is even more beautiful, old, worn and wonderful.

"After all, in those 40 years, it is I who have changed. And Miami, Fl. Think what these 40 years have done to it and its beautiful open bay."

—Miami Herald *Travel section, November 1959*

"It's time that we all let it be known that we're sick and tired of the ruin and loss of things which are our natural heritage. We're no longer little old ladies in tennis shoes. We begin to be a formidable bunch of people; we begin to be a public voice."

—*February 1972 speech to second annual Conservation Night at Fairchild Tropical Garden*

"I object to the term suffragette. Suffrag-ist is a perfectly good ending. Suffragette reminds me of, 'There, there nice little girl. Now just do as you're told dear, and don't bother us.'"

—*February 1974 endorsement of Equal Rights Amendment*

"Why should I sit around and think about my aches and pains? I hate to be bored. I seem to be pretty healthy and I think it's because I'm interested. I'm having a wonderful time."

—*January 1978, interview at age 87,* The Miami Herald

MARJORY STONEMAN DOUGLAS

"We were ushered into a big room in the Capitol. I remember there were men sitting around the walls spitting into spittoons.

"We made it quite clear that we were all born Americans, we were all citizens, that you could not withhold the vote from part of the citizens, that taxation without representation was tyranny.

"We all five spoke. Mrs. [William Jennings] Bryan made one of the best suffrage speeches I ever heard.

"All you could hear was the sound of our own voices and the ring of the spittoons."

—*From 1985 interview at her home recollecting her 1916 trip to Tallahassee in support of passage of the 19th Amendment. (Florida was the only state in the union never to vote for or against the amendment.)*

"It's women's business to be interested in the environment. It's an extended form of housekeeping, isn't it?"

—*Jan. 31, 1983,* Time *magazine*

Marjory Stoneman Douglas in 1995:

On saving the Everglades: "It isn't saved yet."

On writing: "I always wanted to write so I wrote. That's what it is all about. And it ought to be something you want to write about."

On being 105 years old: "I don't know what you ought to feel like at 105 because I've never been 105 before."

On people coming to her for wisdom: "If they do, they will probably be disappointed."

On her lifelong habit of staying up late, working at night, sleeping late in the day, and taking afternoon naps: "I sleep when I choose."

On the most foolish question a reporter ever asked her: "That one is."

GEOFFREY TOMB

Geoffrey Tomb is a Herald *general-assignment reporter.*

Stetson Kennedy

BY WILLIAM ROBERTSON

Writer Stetson Kennedy, in charge of collecting folklore in Florida for the Works Progress Administration during the Great Depression, can tell one hell of a good story.

I was born in 1916 in Jacksonville. I recall my father coming down to Miami, I believe, in the early '20s, probably in a Maxwell phaeton automobile, meaning an open-convertible type thing. He came back to Jacksonville, saying there's nothing down there but a bunch of gators and skeeters. The boom was still going strong when he came back again and brought the five Kennedy kids in the phaeton with him. He was looking all around and saying things like, "My God, what money's done to this country." That's been happening ever since. It's been doing things to the country: Lots more people and fewer mosquitoes and gators.

That was before the hurricane [in 1926]. That was the big one, of course. It took all the faces off the hotels on Biscayne Bay. A black preacher out in the Glades composed a song about the "hairycane," as he called it. It's in my book *Palmetto Country*, I think. It had some good lines, I thought, like:

Great God Almighty did move out on the water
And all the peoples in Miami run.
Ships swam down that ocean.
It was most too sad to tell.
Ten thousand peoples got drownded
And all but twelve went to hell.

So you had the so-called black subculture out in the Glades, cane cutters, passing judgment on the culture of Miami, and that was the verdict.

I went to the University of Florida in Gainesville in the early '30s and stayed about a year and a half. They had no courses in creative writing, although Marjorie Kinnan Rawlings came over one summer and gave a six-week course, which I took. Gainesville had no other courses. I wasn't even allowed to take journalism until the junior year, so I say I invented independent studies by dropping out. I packed a steamer trunk full of books in Jacksonville and shipped it by the Clyde Line ships to Key West—it was the

STETSON KENNEDY

cheapest way to get them there—and then hitchhiked after them to Key West in '35, as I recall. In Key West, the intention was to write.

All told I spent four or five years in Key West. I went back to the university for a time and then returned to Key West. While at the university I signed on with the WPA Writers Project as a junior interviewer at $37.50 every two weeks, the same salary and job title that Zora Neale Hurston signed on with. Even though she had published two novels, she was still glad to get the $37.50 fortnightly.

We had Zora Hurston running around Florida. In those days it was pretty much unthinkable for black-white to travel together, much less male and female black-white. So I had the bright idea, I thought, of sending Zora ahead as a scout into the turpentine camps and the Everglades and whatnot to identify people with a repertoire of folk stuff. That's the way we did it. We would follow with the machine and she would provide us with names and addresses. Although we quite often did some recording together.

The native Floridian and white and black cultures were much more pronounced then than now. They had not been affected by the mainstream, national culture to the extent they have now.

So we were collecting things like this old black fellow saying, "When you in Rome, Georgia, you got to act like it." I told that to Alan Lomax and he thought it was the funniest thing he ever heard. Or a black domestic saying, "I feeds white folks with a long spoon."

I think my first encounter with folklore might have been when I was still in Robert E. Lee High School. I dated this little girl from across the tracks, so to speak. We had no sooner pulled up into Lover's Lane and she started saying things like, "I ain't never done nothin' but catch hell sinst I was hatched." And, "I've already done more livin' than you ever will." So I said to myself I'd better stop what I'm doing and start taking notes. I've been taking notes on a lot of things ever since.

I don't remember too much about Miami on the boom trip, except that all the men were wearing golf caps or straw hats and knickers—the real estate salesmen and so on. My aunts were buying lots in Miami, which turned out to be under water. But coming down as a student the very word "Miami" had this allure for all of us more or less rural, rustic Florida students. I recall we were having a drink somewhere on the beach and this woman came up—young woman—asking us things like, "Do you have the time?" We assumed that to mean she was a professional. We had the time but not the money. All of that was very exciting.

I was enormously struck coming to Miami by the difference first of all in the vegetation, the tropical vegetation. I had already said to myself if I were an Eskimo I would move to Miami. I sort of resolved the same thing. It was time for me to get out of North Florida and go to South Florida because I found the atmosphere and the sunrises and the sunsets and the long twilights much more to my liking. The moment I get as far north as Daytona and start running into the scrub pines and Spanish moss, I start getting depressed. The prevailing intention is to retire somewhere in South Florida, if I can be both near some water and away from traffic jams. That's the dilemma. I don't know if that's possible even.

Palmetto Country was published in '42, and I was living at 1327 SW Fourth Street in a garage apartment. And after living there for some time, I lived on Alton Road, as I recall, just after it passes Lincoln Road, also in a garage apartment. Incidentally, the local historian, Paul George—he has a walking tour of Little Havana and he's in the habit, he tells me, of

STETSON KENNEDY

walking past my garage apartment and telling them, "That's where Stetson Kennedy lived." Not very impressive. I think it's been burned slightly recently. But it had a little balcony in those days and my attire consisted entirely of a tie-on bikini thing made out of parachute camouflage cloth. And I just tied that on and I did all my writing, month after month, in that bikini sitting on that deck on Southwest Fourth Street.

My son was born about that time in Jackson Memorial. He was crawling around under my table and typewriter pulling the hair on my legs before he could walk. His first words were, "Go away, go write the book." Because I was saying constantly to him, "Go away, I'm trying to write a book."

I spent some five years of my life altogether in Miami, mostly during a period preceding World War II and during World War II.

I was at the train station when the Orange Blossom Special and all these trains were coming in. There was one train full of new Army recruits. This fellow, perhaps from the Middle West or somewhere, gets off the train, and he's in uniform and he starts looking in a 180-degree circle, looking at the horizon, the landscape. And he says, "Everywhere you look it's a picture."

WILLIAM ROBERTSON

William Robertson is an editor on the Herald's *national desk.*

MORRIS LAPIDUS

BY JO WERNE

Internationally revered architect Morris Lapidus counts Lincoln Road storefronts, Miami Beach apartments, and the Fontainebleau Hotel among his achievements. He also created bean poles, cheese holes, and the Woggle.

My earliest memory is as a child of about 5 years old. I was not born in the United States. I came here when I was 7 months old and I had to learn English. I had a favorite uncle, my Uncle Harry. . . . We lived close to the Williamsburg Bridge, which was just being completed on the Brooklyn side [of New York's East River]. One day he told my mother, "I want to take little Moises and show him the world." My mother said, "What kind of crazy idea is that." My uncle said, "We will walk to the river and the bridge and see ships from all over the world, so let me take the child."

So he took me out on the Williamsburg Bridge, which really hadn't opened, but you could walk out on it. So we walked out, I got tired, and he picked me up and carried me. Finally, we got to the middle of this, and he said, "Look at it. Look at these ships from all over the world on the wharves, on the Manhattan side, the wharves on the Brooklyn side." And he said "Look at the building, that is the tallest building in the world, the Singer Building.

"Maybe one day when you grow up you'll design a building just as tall, maybe even taller."

THE WOGGLE TAKES SHAPE

Man loved to adorn the place where he was living. That adornment and that shape, because the caves were not made of square shapes, they were meandering. So I began to use meandering forms. I never used a straight line. If I could put a curve in, I'd curve it. Then I developed the shapes, which I called Woggles, whether it was a whole store shaped in a Woggle or an ornament shaped or a display shaped or a thing on a ceiling. I didn't give it the name Woggle. An editor once said, "You're the Woggle designer. Another editor said, "No, he's the cheese-hole designer. He's using round holes all over the place." Another editor said, "I think he's the bean-pole

MORRIS LAPIDUS

designer, because I used slender poles." That became my alphabet of ornament, plus color and plus all the other things I had devised.

THE HOTEL

I designed the Fontainebleau. I had never worked in concrete and I did the whole thing in concrete. The Fontainebleau used all of my theories of curving, sweeping lines, drama, lighting, color, adornment. Everything that I had been using to sell merchandise and it was, of course, a great success.

It was great big islands of carpet in the Woggle shape with beautiful furniture so people could wander around and sit down in these islands. I designed the furniture, which you could never use in a home; it was way overscaled, but people would sit down and feel, "My God, this is luxury." I used color all over the place.

There was never a sign in front of the Fontainebleau, until the Hilton took it over. People just knew where it was. It was probably the most famous hotel in the world.

But the critics were so vehement. I knew them all. They said, "Morris, have you gone crazy? You're designing curved buildings and curved shapes, and we don't design buildings that way." I said, "No, I want to break out of the box."

This criticism lasted until I retired. I said, "You say what you want, but I'm designing for people." Basically that is what I was trying to do all through the years. Design for people. For Godsakes, who are you designing buildings for? The critics? Who the hell are they?

When I got the Fontainebleau, I was still not [living] here. The thing was designed and built in one year. Something that could never happen again. That was 1954. How I did it, I don't know. I designed the interiors, I selected the furniture, I did the structure, I did everything. I made the uniforms for the bellmen and for the maids. I selected the silver and the dinnerware. Everything came through me. I bought $100,000 worth of classic ornaments, which embellished the whole thing.

Why did I make [the hotel] a quarter circle? When I used to travel, I'd get to a hotel at night because I'd go from job to job. I'd often sleep in the train and get off at the next city. When you get into a hotel, a bellman takes you up and there's a long corridor and you say, "Where is my room?" And the bellman says, "Way down at the end." I'd say, "Oh my God." So by putting in a round [corridor] you can't see very far. You may be walking a city block, but it keeps curving. That's why I did it.

JO WERNE

Jo Werne is the Herald's *home furnishings writer.*

BY GAIL MEADOWS

JUDY DRUCKER

Judy Drucker, Miami's premier impresaria, can really drop names.

My life has always been music, it's just that it took me into various fields. My mother was an opera star, so I had this in my home all of my life, and then I was singing with the Miami Opera in 1965. I was in the chorus in those days because I had two little children, babies at home, actually three little children, babies at home and singing in the chorus [when] this wonderful tenor came along called Luciano Pavarotti. I went home and told my husband, "You have to come to a rehearsal because this is a phenomenon"—and incidentally two years later we discovered another phenomenon in the voice of Placido Domingo, who both made, incidentally, their debuts in Miami, which is something that people don't realize.

In 1967 I was getting sort of bored with my existence. I was teaching at Miami-Dade Junior College, which is what it was called then. I was the musical director of Temple Israel and I led a choir of 68 children and did all that plus bringing up three children, but it wasn't enough for me.

Somehow the bug bit me, and being a member of Temple Beth Shalom, went to see Rabbi Leon Kronish, who is a great orator and was a very, very well renowned human being in the whole political structure of Israel.... One day a girlfriend of mine and her husband, Evelyn Lear and Thomas Stewart, who were famous singers of the Metropolitan Opera, prevailed upon me to make a concert at the temple.

I went to see Rabbi Kronish and he went to the board, and of course they thought I was absolutely crazy.

BUT ...
They underwrote me for the first year to the tune of $7,500.... We put on this concert with Evelyn Lear and Thomas Stewart, and it was a big success.

Then I decided to go to New York on my own; I didn't even know what a

JUDY DRUCKER

management was. I didn't know where you go or what you do. In fact, when I used to call and say, "This is Judy Drucker, they'd generally say 'yes dear' or 'yes honey.'" That put me off, so I went out and bought a black suit, and I got on the plane and I walked in and said, "My name is Judith Drucker.". . . I immediately got newfound respect.

I met the famous Sol Hurok and I said, "Mr. Hurok, they're calling me the Sol Hurok of Miami," and in his words he said, "I didn't know I looked so good, and what do you want to do, darling?" I said, "Well, I want to start a concert series." And so he gave me a young boy who was a violinist at Juilliard in those days, and he only cost about $750. I thought that was pretty good. He was from Israel, and so he was my first violinist, and his name was Zukerman.

I started bringing in orchestras on a small level at one point. Mostly we did recitals, because it's so expensive. I knew nothing about grants, I didn't know anything about fund-raising.

I knew nothing about dance and I felt that as long as I'm doing what I'm doing I must as well become a little more diversified. So I went to New York and I went to a performance of the American Ballet Theater. I saw this young man who had just defected from Russia, called Mikhail Baryshnikov, and Gelsey Kirkland appearing in *Giselle*. I just started to cry and realized that there is another world besides opera and voice.

I decided that we had to bring a major ballet company to Miami. I didn't know how to do it. So I bumped into Mikhail's manager; he said it is very simple.

I went to the American Ballet Theater and sat in the office and met [the woman] who was then the head of it, and said, "I would like to bring a ballet company to Miami." She said, "Great, it's $90,000 a week." Well, $90,000 a week! Today it's $350,000 a week. Of course I blanched and said, "OK, I'll see what I can do." It took a few more years after that until it happened.

I was in Philadelphia visiting my cousins. [My cousin Sylvia] invited me to a little reception. Baryshnikov was dancing that evening. When I walked into the reception, Mikhail was sitting on the couch as cute as could be with his jeans and a T-shirt on. In those days he was with Jessica Lange and she was very pregnant. My son was more impressed with Jessica Lange for *King Kong*. I didn't even know who she was.

I sat next to Mikhail and I told him of my desire to bring a dance company to Miami. He was very funny. You will find that most great artists have tremendous senses of humor. He said, "OK, this is how you do it. You have to drink a glass of Peppervodka, and it has to be followed by green onion—a scallion—and if you can do that I'll come to Miami."

So, listen, I sacrificed and I drank the Peppervodka—which I think I still feel—and the scallion. He laughed and he said, "Boy, I better come now."

Well, I brought them in 1980 and I brought them for 11 years straight until Mikhail quit the American Ballet Theater.

When I started bringing dance and major dance companies, I decided to bring the Alvin Ailey Dance Company. We were the first people ever to bring a black dance company to this community —maybe 10 or 11 years ago—and it made a huge success.

I must tell you that they are one of my favorites. Alvin always insisted that the Alvin Ailey Company give one free performance to students. We were sitting there with about 2,500 schoolchildren and it was so beautiful.

You could hear a pin drop. Alvin Ailey was sitting next to me, and

JUDY DRUCKER

the tears were streaming down his cheeks. He looked at me and said, "Judy, this is what it is all about." I never forgot.

CRAZY LIKE A FOX

If I do write a book, it will be called *The Music World and Other Horror Stories*. Then, of course, there is always Mr. Pavarotti, who always seems to develop a flu or a cold about 10 minutes before he's ready to go on stage. We've had many of those things happen, but he always comes through with it. One time at Gusman Hall, when we did a recital with Luciano, everybody was sitting in the audience dressed to the hilt with their gowns on. I came back to give him a kiss, and he said, "*Cara*, sit down." Whenever anybody tells me to sit down I say that I don't want to sit down. He said, "I have a catarrh." A catarrh is a cold. "I can't sing."

Well, you know, you get a numb feeling that starts in from your toes up to your neck. I just stood there and stood my ground and I said, "OK, I understand you must be sick, but just do me one favor please or I'll just kill myself. Just do me a favor. Go out on stage and tell the people you have a cold and tell them you can't sing.

"And try, try one little note. If it comes out, fine, but if it doesn't, you've told them you have a cold." He said, "OK, for you, *cara*, I'll do it."

He walked out on stage and I got everybody around me to stand up and scream "Bravo! Bravo!" For about two minutes straight we screamed, and of course his adrenaline started running. He said, "That crazy girl Judy. She make me sing and I have a cold, but I will try."

Well naturally, he opened up his mouth and he sounded like a god, and then we got up again and screamed "Bravo! Bravo! Bravo!" He sang a second song and then a third song, and then he said, "OK, I think we have a concert."

GAIL MEADOWS

Gail Meadows is a reporter and columnist for the Herald's *Living and Arts section.*

WILLIAM KROME JR.

BY KATHLEEN KROG

William Krome Jr.'s father built a railroad to Key West. But he is firmly rooted in the citrus and mango groves of South Dade.

In 1902, my father, who had been working in Georgia and South Carolina as a surveyor and architect for various railroads, was between jobs. He bought a small boat and spent his free time sailing up the St. Johns River.

When he came back to Jacksonville, he heard that Henry Flagler was looking for somebody to survey the southern end of the state with the idea of deciding how to route a railroad from Miami to Key West.

Dad applied for the job and got it, and he came down here. I have his weekly reports to his bosses in St. Augustine, which was the headquarters of what eventually became the Florida East Coast Railroad.

In November 1902, Dad reported, "It's impossible to get a crew to make up a survey crew to go to Cape Sable now. Down here every year, this time of year, the people go tomato crazy. There just isn't money that will hire them away from that." He said when the tomato season is over, "I'll probably get a crew," and indeed he did.

[They made] very complete descriptions of the islands that they went over with the idea of establishing the route that the railroad took. Then he worked under a Mr. Meredith.

[But my father] had been fascinated with the way citrus and avocados could grow in the soft limestone rock. He bought land north of Homestead and planted his own groves. The earliest one was in 1906 while he was working and he continued to put in small groves; five, 10 acres, and come up to supervise them every weekend.

His boss, Mr. Meredith, didn't like this. I have a 17-page handwritten letter from Dad to his father in Edwardsville, Ill., explaining that Meredith said, "Krome, you can't run two jobs at once. Now, either work for the railroad here or go on and run your groves up there." And Dad chose to run the groves.

WILLIAM KROME JR.

When Meredith's health failed, my father was asked to come back. He did. He was in charge of the construction of all the bridges from Long Key south. Meredith was in charge of the big Long Key viaduct; the rest of them [were] under my father.

MODEL T SCHOOL BUS

The first school I went to was what's now the Neva King Cooper school. It's not like the schools of today. We lived on Avocado Drive. Between us and the school, there was about a mile of solid woods. The rest of it—there were roads, almost as many roads in those days as there are now.

The knighted county commissioners thought that they only had two main purposes: one was to make roads and the other was to make schools. I wish that they would go back to that now.

The roads weren't very good, but it was easy to make them with the soft limestone, which is excellent road-building material. Most of the roads that are here now, including Quail Roost and Eureka, were here in 1920.

Eureka went past Lawrence Pope's place, which is a mile west of us. And Larry Pope was a character. When [the road pavers] wanted right-of-way past Larry's property, he wouldn't give it to them, so they asphalted the road up to his property, didn't do anything in front of his property, and on the other side continued doing it just to show him. They didn't know it but nothing in the world tickled Larry Pope as much as that. He thought that he'd really done something.

I remember when the first school bus came. I was going to junior high then, I guess. It was a Model T Ford with a rickety wooden body on it. It would come around and pick us up. There weren't all that many pupils for them to pick up. But the class that I was in was the largest class that we'd had. We graduated in 1931 and regarded ourselves as the elite, I think, and there were 28 of us in the graduating class. That was the biggest class they ever had up to that time.

The people who came down here—and they came down almost a generation before me in the early 1900s—came from all over the United States and brought more culture with them than you might believe. They had the Long View Women's Club, and they gave recitations and all kinds of things.

There was quite a bit of community work. My mother participated in some, but she was frank to admit that she had enough to do raising her family and the groves.

[My father] was always a community leader. And then, as now, if you are that type of a person, there will be other people who will want to take potshots at you. I was too young to know. Mother said that. It never worried Dad. If it did, he certainly didn't let me know it, but it worried Mother a little bit.

In 1914, which happened to be the year that I was born, they found citrus canker in the upper part of the state and almost at the same time at the Griffin brothers' nursery on the other side of Quail Roost.

The Griffin brothers got their trees from a nursery in northern Florida, and it's generally agreed that's where the [canker] came from. The only way you could get rid of the canker, which was not a fungus but a bacterial disease, was to burn the trees. My father was in charge of it, the eradication down here.

How Dad stood it, I don't know. I played in the groves and played in the woods, and I remember a group of men would come in in the morning and go into one of the buildings that my father had and come out in white coveralls. They had knapsacks and sprayers that had kerosene in them. They

WILLIAM KROME JR.

would torch the trees and kill them completely. There was some opposition to that, you can bet.

NAMING KROME AVENUE

Dad bought the land on the east side of what is now Krome Avenue and the north side of what is now Avocado Drive—and the west side of that, too. Avocado Drive went north to that intersection, then west. It didn't go east at that time.

The two corners on the south side belonged to a man who worked for Dad from Vermont, as I recall. [He died] when [his boat] was blown out to sea. Dad handled his estate for his relatives in New England, and as long as there were these two parcels of land, he bought them. There was never any question as to the propriety of it. In those days land went for very little. So there were four corners that Dad owned and it was known as Krome's Corners. The road ran out there and before too long it was extended north. It was natural to name the road that went to Krome's Corners, Krome Avenue.

It had the name Krome Avenue in the '20s, but in the '20s speculation fever affected South Dade, too, and [Dad sold] to a group that he knew; he knew the principals. They were the best people in the Homestead area and they immediately started developing, putting in wide roads and sidewalks and all those things right through the groves and before they got to pave any of the roads, when they were just impassable piles of rock and so on, the hurricane came and blew everything, including [the] land boom, away.

These people, honorable men, had no way of paying what they owed for the land, and it all eventually came back to us.

KATHLEEN KROG

Kathleen Krog is a member of the Herald's *Editorial Board.*

BY RICK HIRSCH

MAURICE FERRE

Maurice Ferre, former mayor of Miami, brought the city closer to his vision of "Manhattan South." He currently sits on Dade's Board of County Commissioners.

I guess my earliest remembrance of Miami was 1939. I was flying up to New York on a Pan American Clipper that landed at Dinner Key. I was 4 years old so I was a child, but I do remember the excitement of being on a water plane and this big plane landing, getting off in Miami.

I have a very clear memory of what Miami was in the 1940s and it really was a fairly sleepy, wonderful, relaxed, laid-back vacation area. It was very beautiful. I remember, for example, U.S. 1 being lined with trees all the way to the University of Miami, banyan trees, big banyan trees. It was a two-lane road, U.S. 1 was. I remember when those trees were all cut and all the uproar about it.

In 1955, Mercedes and I married. She was our next-door neighbor on Brickell Avenue and I was 20 years old and she was 19. Our parents agreed that it was all right to marry, and it was typical of Latin families. We got engaged. I remember the engagement party at the Surf Club in 1954 on Easter Sunday. We got married in 1955.

Q: Had you been set up by your parents?

No, no, no, no. It was [a] spontaneous thing. Mercedes and I met each other. She was the next-door neighbor and I heard that there were three beautiful Venezuelan girls next door. It was a beautiful house, which was the Santa Maria. I lived in Dr. [Henry] Jackson's old house, which my dad had bought and my mother spent a fortune redoing to my father's chagrin, but she had made a very beautiful house out of it. Modernized it and cleaned everything up and tore down all these walls and made bigger rooms and what have you, and so we had an old colonial revival house, Dr. Jackson's house, on Brickell Avenue.

Q: Can you describe what downtown looked like in 1963 when you became president of Maule Industries?

MAURICE FERRE

Yeah, in 1963 the only thing that had happened since the Depression, since before the Depression, was the Southeast Building . . . and my father always was a real visionary, saw very clearly that something was going to happen. . . . He bought the Mayflower House, where Pan American Airlines had their downtown operation and that eventually became the One Biscayne Building, and then he bought the 100 Biscayne property, which is just a couple of streets up on Biscayne Boulevard, and already in the 1960s, he was dreaming about all these buildings. He thought that Miami would eventually boom and so he wanted to be in the forefront.

He wanted to have Miami's tallest building. So he went out and built —I think it was seven feet taller than the courthouse, without counting the antennas, and it was a wonderful experience for me to watch all of this come about because my dad started it, he did most of the design himself and started the building without a mortgage. He just was gonna build this building, so he signed a contract with Frank Rooney and they started pouring concrete, and before you know it, it was up to the 18th floor. Finally, he worked something out with Equitable and got a mortgage for the building. But it was a very risky thing to do because it was one of the first buildings in the country that was mixed use. He had 20 floors of office and 10 floors of residential.

I tell you all this because you know a lot of people say that I have a vision for downtown and that I'm the architect of the modern Miami and all that kind of a thing and that's an exaggerated thing, like most of these things are, hyperbole and all that. But I come by it legitimately, I come by it through my father. My father was the great dreamer of wanting to develop downtown Miami. Unfortunately for him and for the rest of the Ferre family, that didn't work out and as you know when Maule Industries went bankrupt in 1978, we lost, my father lost, all of the properties and therefore, in effect, I've been able to do in the public sector what my father began to do in the private sector, which is a great satisfaction to me.

[My father was] in the rich tradition of Florida land speculators, and made a tremendous amount of money. If I look back, my guess is that over a 20-year period he probably accumulated $200 million worth of real estate, but I mean $200 million in 1970 dollars.

Q: Your period as mayor was obviously one of tremendous change in Miami in a lot of ways.

1973-1985. Twelve years. Describe the physical structure of the city.

Well, in 1973, the only new thing in town was my father's building. There was nothing else. . . . I think the last big stuff that was done was done in 1928, 1930 and this was in the 1970s. I think it was 40 years of nothing other than Southeast Bank Building done in downtown Miami.

Q: That was the First National Bank of Miami?

Yeah, it was the First National Bank and it was a 17-story building, on Biscayne Boulevard. . . . Miami was a sleepy little town. It had 300,000 people, mostly white Americans, Anglo or whatever, however you want to designate it, a very large Jewish community, a very large Greek-American community, a fairly prominent Lebanese community, but mostly Southern. Miami was mostly people from Georgia, South Georgia, a lot of people from Alabama, some people from Mississippi and the Carolinas, but it was mainly Georgians. And those were the people you ran into in the Miami Club, you know.

That was a non-Jewish, non-Hispanic, nonblack, nonfemale, white, Anglo-Saxon world. That was the establishment of Miami. In

MAURICE FERRE

1973, the Cubans had already been here for 11 or 12 years but they were really struggling just to make it. Those were tough years.

Miami was in the process of changing from a caterpillar to a butterfly, but it was a metamorphosis. It was really some very interesting things. I saw two things that I think 12 and now 20 years later was my contribution to the community.

One was, for Miami to really be a major city it had to have an important downtown area and that included Brickell Avenue. I saw Brickell as part of Miami. And that was kind of like the engine that pulled the train.

My second clear understanding or vision of all this was that Miami was really going to become a major center of trade and international commerce and we really had to focus on that.... So we created the Trade Fair of the Americas and brought down Mrs. Carter and the president [of] Ecuador.... In a two-year period I visited 16 presidents of Latin America.... It helped that Jimmy Carter was president and I was a Democrat and was active in his campaign.... I was able to use my Democratic Party, presidential credentials in the Carter administration, for the benefit of Miami because I had an open-arms reception at every embassy in Latin America and I took advantage of that and we really traveled. In 1975 I was able to convince [Florida Governor] Reubin Askew along with Eastern Airlines to take the Bicentennial trip and we went down to Venezuela and Colombia. So those years, and I would say really starting in '75, '76, '77, those late '70s [were] really the time that we concentrated greatly on two issues: (1) developing the downtown Miami area and (2) internationalizing Miami.

RICK HIRSCH

Rick Hirsch is the Herald's *deputy city editor.*

Dr. Jean Jones Perdue

BY NANCY ANCRUM

Dr. Perdue was one of the nation's first woman cardiologists in the 1930s. She founded the Miami Heart Institute and doctored a community into good health.

As I finished my training at the University of Virginia, my brother, Dr. T.W. Jones, who had started research of rheumatic heart disease in Boston, was teaching at the Harvard Medical School.

Rheumatic fever was the most common cause of heart disease in New England during the '20s. There was very little of it [in] Florida, and he decided to try to send some children [here] to see if they would improve.

They approached me in the spring of 1933, asking if in the fall I would come. I was finishing an assistant residency in medicine at the University of Virginia.

I said that my husband-to-be was finishing a residency in ob-gyn at Duke, so I said I'd have to get him to come up to Virginia [the] next weekend and we'd talk it over.

So he came and he said, "You'll only promise to do it the one year with the children, and if we get married before you go, you can go."

I came to Florida [in] early December 1933. My husband brought me here, and he had to go back and be on this train by the first of January. He got me established down here, a place to live, and left me two days before the first of the year.

I saw in the paper about a football game. So I gathered up some children in the neighborhood and went off to the first Orange Bowl football game.

I went to work the second day of January 1934, having taken my boards in November and got my license before I came.

There was only one hospital on Miami Beach at that time, St. Francis, which was where the children were being cared for in the studies being done. There had been much publicity in the North [about] the studies that some of the top cardiologists in the country would visit to see what we were doing.

The nuns became my family, and because they respected my brother, they immediately began

DR. JEAN JONES PERDUE

recommending me to people. I became a physician to many of the richest people in this country who came here for the winter. I still have some of the connections, all these years, with those families.

I also became knowledgeable that south of Lincoln Road, which was a beauty spot—it was lovelier even than Worth Avenue in Palm Beach—there were many indigent old people. So I started working with some of the indigent older people on South Beach.

With the publicity about these children being brought here, there were many people in the country and other places who came to Miami Beach thinking the sunshine and ocean were going to cure them. They were young adults, fathers and mothers, some families. Many of them didn't have money. So I had to start up for some way to get funds for them.

I worked with Miami Beach social services right from the start, and became a part of doing community work.

I immediately joined the Dade County Medical Association. My father had always been active, and I joined the Virginia Medical Association as soon as I took my boards when I graduated.

I think one reason I was accepted so well by the physicians locally was because my brother had sent these children here and had spoken to the Florida Medical Association. So they knew him, and they knew why I was here. Therefore as a woman physician I had no problems being accepted into the medical profession.

[This] was a godsend to me because with my pregnancies in 1936 and '39 and again in '41, I had to get other doctors to help with my practice. They were always willing to do so. When I would get back to work in two weeks, my office would be full again.

The first month that I practiced —and this was the Depression—I collected $660. When I wrote this news to my husband at Duke, he and all of his associates felt I'd hit a gold mine. So I guess maybe that started him thinking that maybe this was the place for us to stay.

NANCY ANCRUM

Nancy Ancrum is a member of the Herald's *Editorial Board.*

Psalms, Songs, and Salvation

Sustaining the Spirit

HISTORIANS

Nancy Ancrum: What about religion here? What about churches, temples . . . that could sustain anyone anywhere, but what about here, specifically?

Howard Kleinberg: . . . The roots of this community's history are based in our churches. (Our temples didn't start until later so let's just stick with churches.) Both the white community and the black community—they seem to have grown and, I don't want to use the word "control," but been influenced, I guess is the best word, by religion and by the church. In the later days of this community and all the problems we've had, the churches and the synagogues have been the one constant that has managed to bring us together.

Dr. Paul George: I kind of think that's an American pattern; I really do. The leadership, the civil rights movement coming out of churches; people just turning to churches in times of turmoil no matter where you live. Synagogues, mosques, whatever.

Dr. Juan Clark: Certainly for the Cuban refugees, the churches were crucial at the very beginning. The role that the Catholic Church initially played when Monsignor [Bryan] Walsh was a very important person. In actually promoting their welfare, physically, materially . . . but also on the spiritual side was a very important thing that we have there, our Lady of Charity shrine there that is a national shrine. . . . It has played and is still playing a very important role in uniting and, as you said, in times of crisis bringing everyone together.

Arva Moore Parks: . . . Growing up in Miami, it was very much more of a Protestant town because there were so many Southerners here . . . and there weren't a lot of Catholic churches and I think what the Catholic Church has done with the arrival of the Cubans and with the Haitians is just one of the great Miami stories. . . . That speaks to our diversity again. If you look at our first City Council people—a lot of them after the initial Flagler group, they're very Southern, yet we had Catholics elected, which is pretty interesting when you look at Georgia, the history of Georgia or you pick up North Florida—that would not have been a common thing to have happened.

Howard Kleinberg: When I talk about the value of the churches, I think in addition to taking care of its own flocks, I think the churches have crossed lines and reached into other neighborhoods in areas and religions; not to proselytize but to work with.

A perfect example to me, being Jewish, is 1939; we've got the *St. Louis* floating off the coast of Miami Beach and a rally was held in Bayfront Park—not started by the rabbis but by Christian ministers: Baptists, Methodists, and all that. There were thousands of people in Bayfront Park holding a

HISTORIANS

rally to pressure the United States government to take the Jews in off the *St. Louis*. Who would expect that in the South in 1939?

Arva Moore Parks: Also in 1896—I think it's that early—the *Miami Metropolis* editorially took on the community for having blue laws that shut down the Jewish merchants.

Howard Kleinberg: . . . The Jews, the first Sunday of the city of Miami, the Jews opened their business. Sunday wasn't their Sabbath. They all got arrested because there was a blue law and the judge wasn't quite sure what to do; he had to find them guilty but he only fined them about a dollar or something like that. The *Metropolis* had an editorial campaign—

Arva Moore Parks:—"Lighten up"—

Howard Kleinberg:—If the Jewish Sabbath is on Saturday, let them close on Saturday and be open on Sunday, but they couldn't be open both days.

Arva Moore Parks: For the time and place, that was a pretty open attitude about it. . . .

There's a certain spirit here and I think it's optimism; it's looking to the future; it's all this starting over. And I was real pleased when Bill Clinton, President Clinton, used that, talked about the spirit of Miami [at the Summit of the Americas] and I have a spirit of Miami file, too, where I've collected all the things people have said about the spirit of Miami. After the Christmas night fire in 1896, the *Metropolis* said the spirit of Miami is at work, or something like that; Miami arises from the ashes. I think, after our great tragedies, after the '26 hurricane, there were all these references to the real spirit of Miami, the pick-up, dust-yourself-off, start-over-again spirit of Miami.

Nancy Ancrum: Where do you find that spirit of Miami, Dorothy?

Dorothy Fields: I guess I first started thinking about it when I got a chance to interview Mrs. Annie Coleman, who was a pioneer, who worked for D.A. Dorsey and was from Quitman, Ga. Came here as a young bride, I guess, in the '20s. She was, for 25 years, president of the Friendship Garden and Civic Club. The purpose of that club really was not so much gardening, although they provided the flowers and the landscaping for the schools, the black schools. But they were actually in cahoots with some of the women at white Temple Methodist Church. As it turns out, the husbands of the white women were actually city officials who, by day in fact, enforced laws against blacks and at night, too, but their wives, with their compassion and their concern for the black community, worked with Mrs. Coleman and the Friendship Garden and Civic Club to make changes, and they were very successful.

BY
JON O'NEILL

GIAN CARLO VACCHELLI

Gian Carlo Vacchelli, a student at Riviera Middle School, was born in Peru in 1981. He has a disease that makes his bones very brittle and stunts his growth. It's no big deal.

Q: OK, tell me a little bit about what it was like when you first came here.

It was a big transition coming to Miami. But then I said because it was fun and I got to learn English and they had, I had time enough to learn English because many people knew Spanish so I had time enough, you know, to talk my own language and to be able to learn English.

Q: Why don't you want to leave?

Because Miami is a home to me. I like Miami. You know, it's so nice to wake up in the morning and look at the sunrise and, you know, I just like Miami. It's a big city.

Q: You like to party, Gian?

Yeah. I don't know; that's the kind of person I am, I guess. I'm used to Miami . . . every night, Monday through Sunday there's a party night, you know. Music, dancing, sports, anything in Miami, every night. Everywhere you go.

Q: You like to be entertained?

Yeah, especially with sports, though. They mean a lot to me from Miami, my Heat, my Dolphins, my Panthers, even though for some people it's not a lot, for me it's a part of me.

Q: Tell me a little bit now about when you were born with your condition. What did the doctors say?

Well, the doctors said I was going to die. I didn't know all this, of course. My parents told me this. I wasn't conscious when I just was born. But my parents told me that the doctors say I was in a bad way, but my mother was suffering a lot because, as you know, my birthday is eight days before Christmas and the doctors said I wasn't going to make it to that Christmas.

Q: You're very different from a lot of kids.

No, I'm not. The only difference between me and the other kids is that I move on wheels. They move on legs; but trust

GIAN CARLO VACCHELLI

me, wheels are better. You can do much more things. You can make a good curve.

Q: Do you ever miss, like when you see kids play basketball—?

Yeah, I miss it. But to tell you the truth, I always dreamed to be a basketball star. I would love to play that game.

Q: When you think like that, what do you think?

I look at life, I look at it in a different approach. I want to be a coach of the NBA. Many people have told me I can't do that, either. Only 1 percent of the Americans are able to be basketball coaches, but that doesn't keep me down. I'm going to pursue my dream if it's the last thing I do.

Q: OK, tell me a little bit about how you look at life, Gian Carlo; what do you think about just life in general. . . ?

Life is a video game. I have a Sega Genesis and I know I'm jumping off the subject but I'll get back into it because I'll tell you what, life is like [video games], because you can have stages, and I think you have obstacles in life and I think life is a video game. You have life, then you have to pass a goal, and in the video game your goal is to catch the princess. Well, here your goal is to do whatever you set your goal. This is better than the video game, because in life you get to set your own goal. On the video game they set your goal for you. That's the only difference. And like my old saying goes, and I'm sure you've heard it before, "I don't have no problems; I only have difficulties." And I've said that before. I'll never stop saying it.

Q: Now, do you still have problems with your bones sometimes?

Oh yeah.

Q: You would break bones?

Yeah, and I still do. But my doctor says as I grow more up, you know, as I grow more, my bones will break less. And it still hurts when I break my bones. I'm not gonna tell you I'm out, happy, dancing the lambada, but it still hurts. But it's not a difficulty anymore because it has its good things. To tell you the truth, breaking a bone has its good things. They give you everything; you don't have to fix your room, you don't have to do anything. You can't move a muscle. And sometimes you can't even go to school for a couple of days. So it has its good things, I mean, don't tell my teachers; I hope they don't hear it. But it has its good things and it has a lot of bad things, but I haven't broken a bone in a year now. I'm happy; an all-time record and I hope it keeps up.

Q: You said "in my life something bad almost never happens." Do you really feel that way?

Yeah. Almost never. Every day I ask the Lord to give me a good day and not every day it happens. But most of the days it does. Sometimes I want to trade; sometimes I go, "Oh God, I want tomorrow to be a good day because the Heat plays and let today be a bad day, if you want." And I did that today, you see, I go, "God, let tomorrow be a good day because they got a big game against the Falcons and let today be a bad day" and today wasn't a very good day. So I expect tomorrow to be, give me what He promised . . . Oh, man, I was going to tell you something.

Q: No, go ahead.

Oh, sorry. You know, you may think this is weird, too. I'm in the choir group at school and you may be asking what does this have to do with what we're talking about? Well, I'll tell you now because when we sing a song, in my head, I picture basketball. You know how they do and they show the players and when they're singing the song and when they show the producer and they show the guy that . . . that's what I picture in my head. I picture Glen Rice shooting a 3,

GIAN CARLO VACCHELLI

I picture me as a coach hugging the players, holding the championship in my hand, especially basketball when I hear a song.

Q: What do you have trouble with in school?

Math. Reading comprehension. I'm not very good at reading comprehension.... I'm not a good writer. My writing's not neat enough.... School is fun, but school is tough.

Q: And how did you manage to learn English so fast?

Luck, luck, really. Big-time luck. Give all the credit to Miss Millie. You know her? My teacher at Auburndale [Elementary School]. Give all the credit to all my teachers at Auburndale.

Q: How do you stay so up, Gian Carlo?

It's hard. All the bad news I get in school, boy? You wouldn't believe it. It's hard; it's darn hard.

Q: How do you do it? How do you do it?

I don't know. Miami keeps me up, I guess. All the partying and the fun of boating.... Let's dance the lambada. I mean, what can I tell you? Miami keeps me up. The Heat, the Dolphins, the Panthers, the celebrating, the adventure, everything keeps me up here.

Q: You really do feel that way, don't you?

Yeah, I really do. And I may not be the smartest person in school but I am a terrific human being. Inside. And I guarantee you that.

Q: How do you know that?

'Cause I feel it. And I feel it, Jon. Is this a great way to close it off? It's like a movie, boy. I'm getting emotional here, sir.

Q: Well, you really do feel that. You do have something special inside.

Oh yeah. No doubt about it.

Q: What's there?

Love. For everyone.

JON O'NEILL

Jon O'Neill is a Herald Neighbors *reporter.*

BY
CYNTHIA CORZO

LUCIANO GARCIA

From a beach towel to having it his way.

I arrived in the United States on May 28, 1980. I remember that we left from the port of Mariel, in Havana, on the 27th, about 8 or 9 P.M. About seven or eight hours earlier, I arrived at Mosquito Beach. It was a very peculiar site because it was like a waiting room for those about to board the boat.

One of the memories that comes back to me is the food. They were handing out small cardboard boxes with white rice, scrambled eggs, and a slice of bread. I swapped my box with white rice and scrambled eggs for a slice of bread. All I ate that day was two slices of bread.

We set sail and it was a mess. That night, there was an awful storm and everyone on the boat started vomiting. I didn't, because all I had eaten was my two slices of bread, but everybody else was throwing up eggs and rice. It was terrible.

The vessel, the *Jorge Alberto*, was a fishing boat with room for about 18 people, according to a navy official who spoke to me. Thirty-nine people were aboard. That's part of the memories one has of the trip.

At dawn the following day, we saw the sea around us was light green in color, and all of a sudden we saw this huge Coast Guard ship coming out of nowhere. Everybody burst into applause. The Coast Guard guided our boat to Key West, where we finally docked.

After the stormy night, after all that sea water had flooded the boat, my black trousers had turned white with the salt. So were my shoes and blue shirt, which I've kept to this day at home, as souvenirs. My shorts, my socks, all those garments are stored away at home.

BEACH TOWEL EXPECTATIONS

The picture I had of Miami came from a beach towel I saw at my grandfather's home when I was a child. One of my uncles, who came to Miami in the 1950s, brought this beach

LUCIANO GARCIA

towel back as a present for my grandmother. It showed the Florida peninsula, with a lot of flamingos walking across it. It said, "Florida, U.S.A." or something like that.

I thought of Miami as a beach town like Santa Maria del Mar, that is, flanked by water, beach homes, sand, coconut trees. Of course, we had seen pictures of Miami but that's the impression one gets of Miami. We didn't know about Dade County, Coral Gables, Cocoplum, Gables by the Sea, we knew nothing about that.

I arrived at Key West on May 28. By then, the Orange Bowl and Tamiami were full. There was no space left for refugees in South Florida. They sent me to Harrisburg, Pa., to Indiantown Gap. I spent 30 days there, going through medical check-up, immigration processing, and so on. When I arrived at Miami Airport, when the plane door opened, we were bused to Rancho Boyero Airport, where a truck pulled up to the plane carrying the stairs and the people walked down and then walked to the terminal or took a bus to the terminal. That's when I saw Miami.

When I left the airport and saw the streets and the buildings, I realized that the beach towel at my grandmother's home was just a feeble image of this great city that opened its arms to us.

I came to this country in high spirits. I said to myself, "If I have to sweep floors, I'll sweep floors; if I have to chop wood, I'll chop wood." I studied journalism in Cuba but never practiced it, because in order to be a journalist in Cuba you needed to be "integrated" [to party ideology] and I wasn't "integrated." I had a very lovely diploma hanging from a wall but I never was able to get a job.

I didn't come here pretending that I was a journalist, but I was lucky enough—and God was with me—to meet some very good people. I always tried to get close to people who would give of themselves, not take away from others. I'm not talking about material things but about the gift of opportunity, the chance for you to show off your skills, your ability to do something.

Eleven years after leaving as a "stinking piece of scum," I returned as a reporter for a U.S. television network [Telemundo] and did some pretty daring reporting for our Miami audience. My reports told some truths that were being kept from our community in Miami.

The boatlift was an injection into Miami's Cuban community. Many people here thought that those of us who stayed in Cuba—for whatever reason—had become Stone Age people. They were shocked when they saw that the boatlift brought writers—good ones, too; painters—good ones; doctors—good ones; engineers, architects, professionals—good people all.

SOURCE OF SUCCESS

First of all, I trust in God. If you place yourself in His hands, everything's possible. When I left Cuba, I placed myself in God's hands. At all times, I let His will guide me in my pursuits. Of course, God says, "Help yourself first, and I'll help you later."

Effort. Time. Dedication. If, in order to succeed, I have to go through a wall, I'll go through it. I may come out the other side bleeding from the head and I may wind up in the hospital. But I will break down the wall and come out the other side. You can't sit down and wait for someone else to break down the wall or lend you a hammer and chisel so you can break the wall yourself. Either you get the hammer and chisel yourself or you knock the wall down with your head.

I have always had the support of my family and have always taken advantage of my opportunities.

LUCIANO GARCIA

The United States is the land of opportunity. I see so many unemployed people, so many people on welfare. I don't understand this. There's a lot of honest jobs you can do, maybe not what you'd like to do—wearing a suit and tie in an air-conditioned office—but you can make just as honest a living working in an office as mowing a lawn, cleaning a house, cooking, or taking care of children.

That's the spirit I brought with me, although I didn't have to do that kind of work, thank God. Your attitude has a lot to do with your success.

After I arrived in the United States, the public relations firm that hired me paid for an American-born English-language teacher for me. She gave me private lessons three times a week for a year and a half. I also went to Miami-Dade Community College. My English at the time was very basic: "Tom is a boy. Mary is a girl," you know, simple sentences.

After living two months with my relatives, I became independent and got my own apartment. I worked, so I had no time to cook during the week. I liked hamburgers a lot and went to Burger King. I learned how to say "Whopper" and "chicken sandwich," "fries," and "Coke." I looked at the menu board, but was afraid to ask for anything else. For a long time, I ordered the same thing: "Whopper, chicken sandwich, fries and Coke." The minute I walked through the door of my neighborhood Burger King, the girl rang up a Whopper, a chicken sandwich, fries, and Coke.

One day I learned the girl spoke Spanish, and from that day on I started to vary my menu. I lost my fear to order other things.

CYNTHIA CORZO

Cynthia Corzo is a reporter for El Nuevo Herald. *Renato Perez translated this interview.*

BY
BILL ROSE

ROXCY BOLTON

Roxcy Bolton, pioneer feminist and a founder of the Rape Treatment Center, Women in Distress, and Crime Watch knows firsthand that "a few women can band together and make a difference."

We led the march down Flagler Street together [in 1973]. I remember the day Rep. Gwen Cherry came to my house. We worked together on many issues relating to women.

[The march] was protesting crimes of rape. It was the first time that women had taken to the streets and 100 of us gathered and marched. I had hoped for at least 50 women to come, and 100 came and I was absolutely delighted. I remember a policeman saying, "Are these the only women in Dade County opposed to rape?" And I said, "Well, is your mother here, is your sister, is your daughter here?"

They weren't taking it seriously. If a woman got off work at 11 o'clock at Western Union and rode the bus home, the police would sometimes say, "Why was she getting off the bus at 11:30 at night? What did she do to cause him to do this?" The whole thing was that we wanted a rape treatment center.

I went to [County Manager] Ray Goode before I went to the the County Commission.... I remember going in and saying, "Mr. Goode, I want a rape treatment center at Jackson Memorial Hospital." And he said, "Is there another one in the country?" And I said, "No, sir. Ours will be the first and they will pattern theirs after ours.

"Let me ask you this, Mr. Goode. What happens when a person is burned in Dade County?" I already knew this, you understand.

"Oh, Mrs. Bolton, we have the finest burn center in the country at Jackson Memorial Hospital." I said, "That's what kind of rape treatment I want. I want the best."

So I said, "Will you support this before the County Commission and put me on the agenda?" And he said, "Yes, I would. I can see the need for it." Right away, he was so smart.

I called [Dade state attorney] Dick Gerstein and I asked him if he

ROXCY BOLTON

would come and support the rape treatment center at Jackson and he said, "You bet I will." And I said, "Dick, I want to have female psychologists there to work with the rape victims." And he said, "I'll support that."

Well, I went that day and gave my pitch and told all the examples and how you went through it all and Dick hadn't arrived yet, and those doors always had a little squeak when they opened up in the back behind you, and so I kind of glanced and, thank God, that was Dick Gerstein walking in the door at just that moment. He came in and supported the rape treatment center, supported female psychologists at Jackson Memorial Hospital. It passed unanimously.

BILL ROSE

Bill Rose is the editor of the Herald's Tropic *magazine.*

BATTLEGROUND NO. 1

I already had my family and the kids growing up in Nashville and Tuskegee. They had been exposed to segregated schools, but they were model schools. One affiliated with Fisk University and the other with Tuskegee Institute. They were excellent educational facilities at that time, but when we came here, we checked to see where the three kids would be enrolled in school. We were assigned to Poinciana Park Elementary School. It was not even a permanent school at that time. It was a group of portables on coral rock.

We checked and found out that Gladeview Elementary was about two blocks closer to our home. Gladeview was an all-white school, and we were told that we could not send the kids although the school decision had been rendered in 1954, *Brown vs. the Board of Education* in Topeka, Kan.

The NAACP had not been active on this issue. They had been advised by

BY
TANANARIVE DUE

DR. JOHN O. BROWN

This opthalmologist was a clear-eyed optimist.

an attorney to leave it alone, the school board will take care of it. They were going to make advances and they would somewhere down the line voluntarily do this.

I headed to the NAACP immediately and found that Father Theodore Gibson was the president at that time. I asked him what had been done as far as the integration of schools. He told me nothing had been done. I said, "Well look, this is 1956 now, and we are getting behind the times. Something should be done in Dade County, and if you are looking for somebody to file a suit, then here, I am offering my kids here. We are ready to do it."

So we got together. He had a son by the name of Theodore Jr., and a school suit was filed representing six black kids in Dade County.

Well, the suit was immediately thrown out by the federal judge, saying that we had not exhausted all the administrative remedies. I can remember distinctly

DR. JOHN O. BROWN

an editorial that was in the *Herald* agreeing with the judge's decision that we had not exhausted all administrative remedies and this was not something that should go through the courts. My oldest boy —who was on the school suit—by the time this suit was settled, he had finished Harvard.

BATTLEGROUND NO. 2

There was a group of us around that time that realized that only a handful of people were involved with the legal cases that were presented by the NAACP . . . so we decided that we would look for an organization, which would involve the commitment and the action of a number of individuals. There was a small, liberal group from Miami Beach who pursued this and found the organization that they thought could represent us, and that we could build upon. That was Congress of Racial Equality.

To begin with, CORE was predominantly white, the local chapter was. I will never forget our first project. We decided just to test and find out how things were. We knew exactly how they were, but CORE always believed in testing to validate our beliefs.

This was in 1959, I guess. The tests we had and the sit-ins we had here in Miami were before the sit-ins in Greensboro, N.C. The difference in the two sit-ins is the fact that ours was formed by adults, black and white, and the sit-ins in Greensboro were done by students.

Our first project for sit-ins started with W.T. Grant's in downtown Miami. We went in there and I think we must have had about 30 people, over half of those were white. We would sit at the lunch counter, and they would immediately close the lunch counter down and start cleaning around us, mopping the floors and everything. They'd make it so uncomfortable for us that we would get up and move away, but then we would come right back and sit in again and then they would close the lunch counter for the entire day.

From W.T. Grant's we went to F.W. Woolworth. We went to the lunch counters at Jackson-Byron's at that time and then we spread to the Royal Castle. Then there was a place called the Rebel Steer on 95th Street and Seventh Avenue, and there was another place called Muggie's over on 36th Street across from Jackson High School. At least once or twice a week, we would be sitting in in these places. Surprisingly enough, the police would not interfere with us. In fact, they did more to protect us and to keep other people from interfering with us. . . . A new Royal Castle had opened down on Biscayne Boulevard, and we went in there, there must have been 20 or 30 of us, so we sat down. We ordered the hamburgers standing up, and as soon as we got the hamburgers we sat down, and of course the manager went haywire and called the police. The police wanted to know what the problem was. He said, "Well, these people are eating hamburgers and sitting in here and they know better."

The police wanted to know where we got the hamburgers. We said he had sold them to us. So the police said, "If you sold them hamburgers, then you have no right to complain. You made money off these people." And the police wouldn't do anything.

After we had eaten those hamburgers, we knew we couldn't get any more, so we left. From that moment on, each time we went into Royal Castle as a group, no one would sell us hamburgers. What we decided to do was to have about 20 or 30 people in cars outside, and one person would go in and order about 20 or 30 hamburgers. They would sell us the hamburgers and the manager or the chef would say, "My goodness, somebody is going to have a party tonight." And we would say, "We certainly are."

DR. JOHN O. BROWN

We would take the hamburgers and go out and distribute it to the people in the cars and then we would come in with the hamburgers and sit down again. It became almost like a joke to us, apart from seeing these people get so upset about our sitting down with hamburgers they had sold us.... We had to have a little bit of humor in some of these things.

SOME RESULTS

To this day I don't how they named me to be a part of the Community Relations Board [in 1963] because I was the antagonist more than anything else.

We did some negotiating with individuals, business owners, and restaurant owners. The mayor of Miami, [Robert King High], strangely enough was so-called liberal, and pressure had been brought on him to get involved in this. He was more or less on our side.

They would bring some of the restaurant owners together and 10-cent store owners together. The Royal Castle agreed to start off by desegregating one of its lunch counters. Then they said, "We'll see how this one will fare. And if we don't have any incidents, then next week or so we'll desegregate another one and we'll do that till we get the whole chain."

After the first two were desegregated, there were no incidents, and they said what the heck are we arguing about anyway. This was before [the] public accommodation law was passed. So we felt we had really accomplished things around here as far as public accommodations were concerned.

TANANARIVE DUE

Tananarive Due is a reporter and columnist for the Herald's *Living and Arts section.*

Mark King Leban

BY SAM TERILLI

He lawyers out in the open— and now he's a Dade County judge.

I remember [during my 1990 campaign for judge]—even though I'm out as a gay male, I wasn't out in the sense that I am now in gay organizations—there was something said that one of the publicists from my then-opponent was snooping around and asking about my sexual orientation as though they were going to use it in some way. It never came to pass and now, five years later, I don't think that would happen now. Things have changed in that small amount of time. It's more accepted. We now have a couple of openly gay judges, and we certainly have some federal judges even now. So things changed there.

I actually "came out" in 1976 in a different sense—in the sense that I admitted to myself that I was gay and to my dear, close friends, my sister, although not my parents. . . . I probably would have taken the next step, but for what happened in 1977, which was the Anita Bryant and Christian Right campaign to repeal—which was the first for Dade County—a human rights ordinance that had been passed, an antidiscrimination ordinance.

I remember thinking that this was a good time to come out because gay rights are being recognized and gays will be protected, and then as soon as it got passed—the ordinance, the Save Our Children campaign came out. That was what she was calling it, Anita Bryant. And then, when I saw the terrible hate that arose as a result of that, I jumped right back into the closet, because here I was a lawyer and I didn't even know how accepting the bar would be to an open gay. And then when I saw that happening, and I was just going into private practice, I decided I couldn't really be out.

Of course, it's been a struggle ever since then throughout the country, but things are definitely

MARK KING LEBAN

better now. Better in the sense that certainly lawyers don't have to fear in every instance being open here in Dade County.

But no, Dade County doesn't have any protection for gays and lesbians in housing, employment, and other areas.... Certainly we should. The idea that we here in Dade County don't need some protection is folly. When I say protection, we're not looking for special rights. Is it a special right to be able to keep a job? I mean, is that so special, because you happen to be a homosexual?

SAM TERILLI

Sam Terilli is general counsel for the Herald.

BY MARIA MORALES

HAYDEE MARIN

Family comes first—in life and in death.

AN AMERICAN WELCOME

When I entered the United States, the Customs agents asked me about the contents of my luggage and I told them they contained my family's silver and jewels. The agent said: "Welcome to the United States," and that made an impression on me, because I realized that this was a capitalist country with many opportunities. I'll never forget that.

I went to Washington... and studied business at George Washington University for two years. I didn't graduate because I decided to come to Miami. I needed to hear the Spanish language. I needed the Nicaraguan community. I needed my family, and I felt very isolated.

It's different in Miami. Miami has warmth. There's a city here, a family, neighbors.

PAIN'S FORCE

My nephew was 13 at the time of his death. When [the Sandinistas] killed him, he was carrying a letter in one hand and an ice cream cone in the other. I was very much affected, because he was only 13 and didn't even know what evil was; he didn't even know about the struggles going on in Nicaragua. When your human rights are violated, your pain forces you to work beyond eight hours a day.

THE CITY MATURES

Miami has grown and has grown up. We're going through a period of xenophobia and racism, when Latin America and the rest of the world are convulsed. Here, you find refugees from all over the world. Many of them bring saddlebags filled with grief, looking for a bit of land where they won't be persecuted, where they can find freedom.

Miami has enriched itself with the professionals who have come here, with the money that has come from Latin America and other parts of the world. Unlike other cities, immigration to Miami is

HAYDEE MARIN

not an economic phenomenon; it's the migration of political refugees, Latin American intellectuals, who have come to make Miami richer.

That's the reason behind this Institute of Human and Labor Rights [at Florida International University], to turn Miami into the center of human rights in Latin America and the world.

For eight years, I worked in Legal Services, from 1985 on. I started as a legal assistant and rose to specialist in economic development. It was fascinating. I didn't know the black community; I didn't know what welfare was. I didn't know anything about welfare and poverty. I came from a well-to-do family, so I never held a job where I could see poverty up close.

I learned a lot from the people who arrived daily, desperate, looking for a little of help. They were overjoyed if you gave them 15 or 20 minutes of your time. When we started working in the economic development of communities, we accomplished a lot. The other work we did was like putting a Band-Aid on a bleeding wound. By developing a community, I gave people a chance to escape from their misery and engage in honest work, and feel like human beings.

I felt very proud when I opened the first grocery store in Ward Towers [in] Liberty City, a community of 300 elderly people, mostly black. How proud the women were to return to the work market, even if only for three hours a day! But just the fact they were selling goods and managing a small store gave them a new lease on life.

I worked with the Mexican migrant community, whom I admire a great deal, particularly the Mexican women, the farm workers. They begin their day at 4 in the morning, preparing breakfast for their children, ironing their clothes, preparing food for their husbands. Once they send everyone off, about 6 A.M., they begin to pick tomatoes, squash, zucchini. Every time I eat a tomato or bite into a zucchini I think of those extraordinary women who go on the fields —even if they're seven or eight months pregnant. They do that to improve the lot of their children.

All these communities have taught me a lot and I feel a great deal of respect for them all.

I've gone picking tomatoes with my Legal Services clients to see what it felt like. They reminded me of Nicaraguan farmers harvesting their crops and reminded me that I often walked past them and never stopped to look at them. I've eaten lunch and dinner at their homes, shared their food. I've gone to baptisms and weddings with them. They opened a world I didn't know and that I got to know only after I became a refugee.

Miami is my home, my world. I love Miami; I admire it. The sunsets, the ride down Ponce de Leon, going to the beach, to the Keys. I haven't stopped loving Nicaragua, but I believe this is now my town and I will remain here. This is where I have learned, wept, loved; where I have found fulfillment as a woman. I'm as much a Miamian as anyone who was born here. I've contributed my grain of sand.

Maria Morales

Maria Morales is a reporter for El Nuevo Herald. *Renato Perez translated this interview.*

BY GRACE LIM

MSGR. BRYAN WALSH

Monsignor Bryan Walsh shepherded 14,000 Cuban children into the United States in the early '60s during Operation Pedro Pan. He will retire after tending this community for 40 years—and get better acquainted with his sailboat.

I believe it was Friday, December 23, [1960]. I received a call from the State Department from a man named Frank Auerbach. He was the head of the visa station, and he said they had information from the American ambassador in Havana that there was a list of 200 unaccompanied minors. Their parents wanted to send them to the United States, and the U.S. government is interested in their being taken care of. But they had to have an agency that was not a government agency, someone not government to accept responsibility. Just a government policy.

He said that "We, the State Department, think that the Catholic Charity is the best one to do this." So I asked how much time I had to give an answer, and he said they needed to know immediately.

I was unable to get hold of the bishop. I had nobody to talk to. I decided to save 200 children from communism would be worth my career. I said, "Yes, we will accept responsibility."

I then asked him when would the first children come and he said maybe on Christmas Day.

I thought "My God, what am I getting myself into?" We had to have facilities for 200 children. He said "You'd better be at the airport to meet them and to see that all the kids come in."

So I called my social workers and asked them to come. We went out and met the three flights from Cuba and there were no unaccompanied children. Meanwhile Immigration at the airport had been alerted by the State Department to be nice to me and to cooperate with me fully and all this kind of stuff.

We were [then] called the Catholic Charity; we are called the Catholic Community Services now. We were a licensed agency, very small, about 10 people and had a few children, and had about 20 beds on Northwest Seventh Street.

I went by Brickell Avenue. There was a place called the Assumption Academy, the corner of 15th and Brickell,

MSGR. BRYAN WALSH

the chapel is now St. Jude's Church. I thought maybe this is the solution. I turned around and went in and asked to see the Mother Superior, Mother Elizabeth. This was a boarding school for girls, but the girls were all home for Christmas so they had beds available. I told Mother Elizabeth we might get 200 kids, refugee children from Cuba, within the next few days: "If I need beds, will you give them to me?" She said, "How can I say No?"

So we went to the airport Christmas Day and nothing. We went on Monday, only six kids arrived.

Meanwhile I had talked earlier to different people about the possibility that we needed some houses and how we might get them. One of the people who offered me a house was Maurice Ferre, who owned a lot of property in Miami at that time. And Maurice had a couple of houses on 15th Road across the street from the Assumption, down towards the bay, where there are high-rise apartments now.

I got the keys and had a look at the houses and thought we should be able to manage. Then I started working with the city inspector to get permission. They were very demanding, we had to change doors, build a fire escape. A few times I felt like throwing the inspector into the bay, but we finally struggled through it.

Each day two or three more kids came.... We were able to gradually take care of them, we didn't get 200 in one day.

When they came in they were extremely nervous, mostly boys, few girls, and in the airport they were extremely nervous because they were subject to some harassment in leaving Cuba. The airport had long delays and so forth. Some of them had come at very short notice, they didn't know what was happening to them.

When they were settled down and calmed down, they spoke to their parents on the phone. Things calmed down a little bit. We had kids with nightmares, kids crying in the middle of the night. We had to do a lot of counseling, but it worked out pretty good.

We thought that this was just a flash in the pan, and that with the embassy shut [in Cuba] there would be no more people coming. But a week or so later I got a call from the State Department asking me to come to Washington. I went up on a Sunday afternoon to meet Mr. Auerbach. He said "Well, we are still interested in the children in Cuba."

I never thought there were going to be more than 200 kids—it was a nice figure. I never imagined it would be 14,000, but it just happened. Eventually we ended up with kids in 35 states, more than 100 charity agencies.

When you are 30 years of age you take chances you don't when you are 65. I suppose that's part of life too. They were very tough times but we survived them and the kids survived them.

LOOKING AHEAD

I was sent here for this job I have today on September 15, 1955 —executive director of Catholic Community Services. At that time, we had about a $100,000 per year budget. Today we have a $20 million budget and 500 in the staff— there has been a little change in the job.

I was 25, one year ordained. The first four years that I was here, the economy of Miami went downhill very fast. We were under severe recession, the United Way was struggling to exist, and Miami was full of empty houses, empty stores, and abandoned houses. The For Sale signs were on Flagler Street from the bridge and Southwest Eighth Street all the way out to Le Jeune Road. Every building had a For Sale sign on it.

In many ways [my job] hasn't changed [in 40 years]. When I

MSGR. BRYAN WALSH

came to Miami in 1955 and was given this job, I was the first priest in this job. The agency had been started about 1931 and I was the first priest directly associated with the Catholic Welfare Bureau and I made a kind of a resolution and spent 50 percent of my time out of the office.

I was pastor of several churches in Miami, always part time. I was filling in the gap when there was nobody to send there. I was pastor of Sacred Heart Church in Homestead from 1957 to 1960. In 1964 I was pastor of St. Agnes in Key Biscayne the same way. In 1965, I was pastor for five years at St. Peter & Paul, the biggest Cuban parish in Miami in those days. There weren't many bilingual priests at that time.

[I learned Spanish] in Puerto Rico. I went there in the late 1950s to learn. I was in my late 20s at the time. Basically I learned it from the boys I lived with.

At the time [that I was sent to Miami] if I was given a choice, I would have preferred a parish. But it turned out that the years I served as pastor it was always a conflict. I thought it was very unfair to the parishioners since I was away so much.

Basically, the church wanted me to be a purebred social worker, and that's fine, because that's what they got. That's what you have today.

I've asked the new archbishop [John Favalora] to allow me to retire this year. He has asked me to stay for a few months, because he is new on the job.

I will fade away, for that's exactly what I'd like to do—kind of fade away. I'm going to have my own apartment here in Miami where I have lived for the last 20 years. I live alone and I want to keep that. Just the thought of moving 5,000 books is enough to make me want to stay! The only community I have ever really known is Miami, so I intend to stay in Miami, keep my apartment and my sailboat.

GRACE LIM

Grace Lim is a Herald Neighbors *reporter.*

BY
DAVE BARRY

GLENN TERRY

Glenn Terry has lived in Coconut Grove for a quarter century, where he will forever be known as the mastermind of the King Mango Strut Parade, a parody of Miami's more famous (and always more tasteful) King Orange Parade.

Q: How did the whole King Mango Strut idea get started? Take me back to the very beginning. What year was it?

Back in '76 I ran for county judge. I stood by the highway drinking rum and Coke with a sign that said, "Vote for Glenn. He looks good in black." I lost.

Q: Hard to believe. Do you know who ran against you?

Richard Alan Schwartz, who now runs a Burger King. He beat me, and the No. 2 guy killed himself.

Q: So you were beaten by a man who runs a Burger King and a man who killed himself.

Yeah . . . lost, but I'm still here. Seriously, I was doing something wrong. I was trying to do the wrong things.

Q: What do you mean by that?

I was practicing law and it wasn't going as well as I'd hoped.

Q: What was the problem?

I didn't wear socks. I got fired by a client once for not wearing socks. I did. I forgot them. It was fashionable not to wear socks. I just started making weird films and doing creative things and I started a band. I always wanted to have a band.

Q: What was the name of your band?

The first band was the Mango Marching Band. We played conch shells. I'm pretty good on a conch shell. I've won a contest on the conch shell.

Q: What style of music were you guys playing?

It was conch. It was very rhythmic. We played conch shells and kazoos. It was a lot of fun. The Goombay Festival was starting and I thought it would be fun to get some white people in the Goombay Parade. I thought it was a real parade. . . . They do have a Goombay band and that's the parade. They march through and that's the parade. So I formed a group of friends called the Mango Marching Band. We wore mangoes on our heads and we marched in the parade.

GLENN TERRY

Q: These were complete, full mangoes that you were wearing on your heads, or did you hollow them out?

No. No. They were two-dimensional. They were like—.

Q: They were cardboard mangoes. You'd have to be some kind of idiot to put a real mango on your head, wouldn't you, Glenn?

I've done that [laughter].

So I started making weird films and I started the Mango Marching Band. I made a lot of mango films like . . . *Mango Maniacs, Last Mango in Paris*, which later became the title of a Jimmy Buffett album . . . then went to LA and tried to make a film for a couple of years . . . I made a movie called *Demonoid*. I play a zombie.

Q: It's hard to believe that you ever came back to Florida.

With memories like that it wasn't easy.

Q: And then you came back to Miami.

Yeah. . . . While I was gone they had like the worst riot that Miami ever had and then the Marielito thing came along. All that happened while I was gone.

Q: So you are clear. You have an alibi for that stuff.

Well, it would never have happened if I had stuck around, obviously. I had to come back and straighten things out and start a parade to give this town some direction, some positive humorous direction. . . . I got the Mango Marching Band together and I thought it was time to go big time, take a big step and get in the Orange Bowl Parade.

Q: You have to apply to get into the Orange Bowl Parade?

Yeah, there's this application process. There's paperwork, photos, audiotape.

Q: It can't be too restrictive because they let Gus Machado Ford in every year.

I remember sitting around [on] my living room floor with a tape recorder playing our kazoos and conch shells and we sent that in. They called us back and said they saw our package and they were considering us to ride in a fire truck. Then they called us back about a month later. I called them and they said, "No, we decided to put a bunch of clowns in the fire truck instead."

Q: So you were replaced by clowns.

Yes, we were. When I got the word it was like November and my [reaction] was, "To hell with them, I'll start my own parade."

Q: "To hell with them, I'll start my own parade," were your exact words?

Yeah. They said you can't be in the parade.

Q: What year was this?

This was the fall of '81. . . . I realized there was a lot more to it than I thought.

Q: What was more to it?

You have to get permission from a lot of people. You have to be nice to the police. You have to convince them that you are not going to start another riot or another Marielito refugee problem with your event. You have to be pretty cool and start slow. I went to the Chamber of Commerce. I wore a suit.

Q: Did you wear socks?

They don't care. That's changed. Now they probably do. I'm sure they do. . . . I lined up my toilet ducks and convinced people that it was a good thing. . . . The main thing you've got to do is get the cops. You want the cops to say it's OK. You hire the cops. They like the extra pay.

Q: Can you remember any of those first groups?

Yeah. I was single then and I was in a group called Miami's Most Eligible Bachelors. We marched with our names and phone numbers on signs. . . . So I've been running the [King Mango] Strut for, it's going to be its 14th year coming up [in 1995].

Q: Fourteen years. Now tell

GLENN TERRY

me some of the memorable units that have marched in the Strut. I remember one year there was an oil spill. . . . the human oil spill that would periodically engulf the crowd.

That was an oil slick that . . . they would bob and weave. They had dead fish hanging off of it. People swimming with their heads just sticking up from the black plastic. That was great. I was in a group called Water Wizards and we wore dunce caps and capes and had divining rods and we found Biscayne Bay and marched into it.

Q: How difficult is it to be a marching unit in the Mango Strut?

You come. You march. You're in.

Q: How big of a crowd do you get nowadays?

The *Herald* has estimated as high as 50,000. We've never had more than 5,000. I know we have never had more than 5,000. The parade is only a block long, so how many people can you put on the street?

Q: So what lies ahead for the King Mango Strut?

Dave, that is hard to say. It will run its course and I'm not sure what that is.

Q: But you'll do it again in our centennial year, 1996?

Yeah, I'm real excited about that centennial. . . . Do you know I was conceived in the excitement of our 50th anniversary?

Q: OK, that makes sense. It can happen.

I try to think, what do these events lead to?

Q: They lead to people like you.

In '46 I was conceived.

Q: Would you say that in all of its history the King Mango Strut has accomplished anything at all useful for humanity?

Oh no. . . . The best stuff is topical stuff. Stuff that recently happened. Like three come to mind. We had a slow chase led by Bart Simpson in a Ford Bronco. . . . The year before that, [the] Lorena Bobbitt Brigade was fantastic. That was really big. That was real strutty material. Half the crowd hated it.

Q: It was very intimidating. You describe it.

It was women supporters of Lorena Bobbitt. They had a sign, the Lorena Bobbitt Brigade, and they had a chant. . . . They had chain saws, they had knives . . . I had a group called the Marching Kennedys. It was right after the William Kennedy Smith rape trial. So we had blue blazers with fake family crests on them. We had champagne bottles and champagne. We kind of marched along as a group of Palm Beach Kennedys in formation. We had a song, but I don't remember it.

DAVE BARRY

Dave Barry writes a humor column for the Herald's Tropic *magazine.*

BEHIND THE BADGE,
ON THE BENCH,
FROM THE DAIS

POLITICS AND THE LAW

HISTORIANS

Dorothy Fields: We've celebrated the 50th anniversary of the first—

Dr. Paul George: Black policeman.

Dorothy Fields: Black patrolmen; they were not policemen. They were patrolmen. They were not allowed to arrest or give a ticket or do any of those kinds of things to white people but they were trained, in secret, in Liberty City to, in fact, be able to help provide some security in the black community.

Arva Moore Parks: I have an interesting personal background because my father was a lawyer and Miami was a very small town then . . . the legal community was such a small community, when you look now at the thousands—

Dorothy Fields: And there were less than 10 blacks, if any, and there were no black women. Gwen Cherry was the first black female lawyer and she didn't graduate from law school and pass the bar until the mid-1960s.

Howard Kleinberg: We've had our share of frontier justice.

Dr. Paul George: Leslie Quigg. Or Dan Hardie. Dan Hardie running for sheriff in 1910. His written platform, if you want to call it that, included the fact that he would arrest suspicious characters first and ask questions later. For our system, that's the other way around.

I really feel the frontier nature and the youth of this community when I study the criminal justice system. . . . One [city marshal] rode a horse, then he rode a bicycle. He was finally thrown off the force because he was inebriated on duty. And he was a dynamiter for Henry Flagler; that was his qualification for becoming the first policeman.

Arva Moore Parks: There wasn't a lot of murder, rape.

Howard Kleinberg: Well, wait, now there's that wonderful 1899 letter written by this guy in Miami to Governor Bloxham. The guy had come down from South Carolina and he was complaining about all the murder and mayhem and he was not going to move his wife from South Carolina to Miami until they cleaned up the mess in Miami—North Miami, it was called.

Dr. Paul George: Now there was a big watershed in terms of things getting more violent in the '20s with the boom. So many new people came and there was such a feeling of dislocation, I guess, on their part that suicides went up, as we know. Homicides did, death by catastrophic accidents.

Howard Kleinberg: [Isn't there research] that showed that the murder rate in the '20s was higher than it was in 1980?

Arva Moore Parks: The other thing that was higher in the '30s and '40s was public corruption.

Dr. Paul George: They got rid of a City Commission because of that in the late '30s.

Arva Moore Parks: We were a wide-open town.

Dr. Paul George: Well, we were because of the whole gambling thing; we were holding onto this in terms of tourism and trying to get back on our feet economi-

HISTORIANS

cally after the demise of the boom in 1926 and the smashing of the hurricane. . . . The Kefauver Commission comes in the '50s.

Arva Moore Parks: That really finished it off.

Nancy Ancrum: What's the "it" that got finished off?

Arva Moore Parks: Gambling.

Nancy Ancrum: What was the Termite Commission?

Howard Kleinberg: It was a corrupt Miami City Commission—

Dr. Paul George:—that was eating away at the liberties of the people; thus the Termite Commission. The *Miami News* mounted a campaign against them, a recall campaign, an exposé.

Nancy Ancrum: Who was this Quigg person?

Dr. Paul George: He was a police chief, for lack of a better term, a real redneck. He was police chief on about three occasions, from the '20s, '21, on and off through the '30s. He ran just as late as '36 an openly racist campaign and was elected.

Nancy Ancrum: Why does crime here reverberate around the world?

Howard Kleinberg: That's because we painted ourselves as a paradise, and any time that there's a snake in paradise it's news. But secondly, we have become the international center.

Dr. Juan Clark: By the way, I wanted to mention something in connection with the famous Mariel crime explosion. Some people . . . actually say the crime rate was already rising significantly when that explosion actually took place. . . . The Mariels simply added another rung to that ladder there.

Howard Kleinberg: That's documented.

Arva Moore Parks: [The Hispanic influence is] a phenomenon to me, again. [In 1980] there were no Hispanic legislators. And in 1990 there were 10. And Bob McCabe often says of all the public institutions—as of we speak this moment, this may not be around for long either—but he's the only non-Hispanic major public administrator in Dade County. We've got school boards, city managers, county managers, FIU, the public administrators. That, to me, is another one of those incredible Miami stories of rapid change.

Howard Kleinberg: One thing about Miami's politics . . . [we] sometimes drift off and look at what we have for politicians now and start talking about "banana republic" politics. When the truth of the matter is, if you do your homework, long before there was a Hispanic presence in politics in this town, we had some of the dumbest, stupidest Anglo administrations that you—I mean, they were comic opera. . . . we could talk about Miami Beach City Council meetings where they were throwing corn-beef sandwiches at each other across the table, you know, and doing the most bizarre things, and all of a sudden we look at our politicians and now they have names that end in "z" and "s" and we blame it all on "banana republic" politics and it's wrong; it's not so.

ARNOLD GIBBS

BY GAIL EPSTEIN

Arnold Gibbs was a Miami police officer during the 1980 riots, which started when four white officers were acquitted of beating a black man, Arthur McDuffie, to death. In three days of mayhem, 18 people died, 270 were injured. Gibbs is now chief of police in Cape Coral, Fla.

BAD NEWS

I was on 63rd Street and Ninth Avenue when the verdict came back. I remember that it was announced over the air on the [police] radio.

I was somewhat shocked to learn what the verdict was, and I knew that from all of the previous hype and media that this was going to be something that would be reacted to, violently. I knew ahead of time.

Shortly thereafter, the dispatcher requested a unit to go by 62nd Street and 13th Avenue to see if they could spot a mob beating a white male or two white males. I heard that request go out, and I left what I was doing and drove one block to 62nd Street and then I went west. As I approached 12th Avenue, I was able to see a crowd of people in the street, and I drove closer and closer.

As I got to 12th Avenue, I could [see] that there was something happening in the middle of that crowd. I started to go across 62nd Street when someone spotted my car and turned around and said something to the crowd. They all looked at me and they charged my car, throwing stuff at it, bottles.

I heard one shot. So I put the car in reverse, backed up across 12th Avenue. As I got out of range of the bottles and rocks, I stopped. Then I realized that there was someone white in the middle of the circle. I got on the radio and advised the dispatcher of what was occurring and to send lots of units down here.

I also advised them to get on the phone and call every radio and television station and advise them to broadcast that Liberty City is an unsafe area and to not drive through. The response I got back from the lieutenant who ran the complaint room at the time was that, "We don't want to start a panic, and we don't want to do that now." I said, "OK, but I'm telling you that this is a start."

They were looting, burning, turning cars over.

ARNOLD GIBBS

They were shooting weapons at anything that moved in that neighborhood—literally. If you happened to be a nonblack, you dare not drive through there at that time because your chances of coming out without being injured or killed were slim to none. And, if you were a policeman, you were certainly going to be a target of violence. If you owned a business, just say good-bye if it was in that area.

It was like the scene out of a movie. The skyline was smoke and fire for miles. You would go down Seventh Avenue, and starting about 58th Street, there were two or three fires on every block until you got to 79th Street.

We took the fire department in there. They couldn't go without police because they got shot at. So we would go in there and get shot at with them, and try to put the fires out. But if the shooting got too bad, we would have to leave unless we could get a SWAT team to go in and find the sniper. We tried to put the fires out, but most were already out of hand by the time we could get there.

Later on in the evening, a decision was made by the division chief to gather up Vietnam veterans with combat experience and put together a team to go into this hostile area. Most people couldn't handle that kind of [violence]. It wasn't cop and robbers; it was war.

So, I volunteered and a few other guys volunteered, and the first time we tried to go in a police car, just a regular police car.

As we crossed Northwest 17th Avenue and 59th Street, the first shot came through the window. Nobody was hit, the window came out and we made a real quick U-turn, turned around, and on the way back out the mirror got shot off of the driver's side. So we took that idea back to the station with us and left it there.

Then, we decided, "Let's get a van that is bulletproof." We also decided—'cause we had people dying—to go get them out of there. So we took the paddy wagons and the bulletproof vests and put them against the windows.

We went down there this time with rifles out the windows on both sides, and we had the people inside the paddy wagon. We took a different route this time, down 12th Avenue.

When we got there, as we approached, looking down the street, you could see the crowd in the middle of the street—about 50 people. They saw us coming when we were a block away and they scattered again and, of course, a couple of shots were fired.

We pulled the wagon over real fast and got out, set a perimeter. Then I saw the one guy first. I remember seeing him lying on his back almost as though someone had placed him there carefully, like in a casket.

He had a long petal rose. At first I thought it was a little rose sitting on his mouth, but it was a [stem] about a foot long with all the thorns on it that had been jammed down his throat. The only part sticking out was the rose. And, the right ear had been cut off. The tongue was cut off a little bit. He had a bullet hole in the side.

Bullets were still flying occasionally, and I didn't want to get off the ground and throw him into a bag—I saw him as dead meat. And, all of a sudden his eyes moved. He looked at me.

I said, "Hey, this one is alive." So [we] picked him up carefully and put him in the truck. Meanwhile, another guy, Manny Gonzalez, spotted a body lying behind the meat market. I would say about 30 yards [away]; they had either dragged him or he had ran. But he was behind the building, off the street. So we didn't know if this guy was dead or alive. So we went over there and sure enough, he was dead.

I remember his head was cut

ARNOLD GIBBS

open. They probably hit him with a hatchet or something. But he was dead. And in fact I said—as the bullets starting getting pretty heavy—"We can't shoot back, we can't see them. Let's just go." And, Manny said, "No, no, let's just take the body." I said, "No, Manny, let's leave it; we'll come back later and get it; he's dead."

He didn't listen to me. He ran over and then grabbed the body and started to drag it. So we all dragged it back to the van.

I was upset over the fact that the trial turned out the way it did. I think it was a miscarriage of justice. I was upset over the way the black community reacted. I wasn't proud at that moment of what was happening. I saw some terrible, horrible things being done to innocent people. I know what anger is; everyone experiences anger and outrage, but to become totally unfeeling, and void of any concern of human life and do that kind of thing to innocent people, the things I saw happening just caused me to experience a sense of humiliation. I just felt bad about being black at that moment.

Some people forget about the pride of being a proud people who endured slavery and a proud people who overcame all of the odds and survived and thrived in this country. Although there is still a lot of ground to cover, blacks in this country have done more than anybody in this country. We have a lot to be proud of.

Gail Epstein

Gail Epstein is a Herald *reporter.*

TOM CASH

BY JEFF LEEN

As DEA special agent in charge, he gave the drug runners a run for their money.

NEW AGENCY, OLD POLITICS

From 1964 to 1969 I was with the Office of Naval Intelligence. Then the U.S. Customs Service was hiring and, of course, the Navy being very frequently in contact with Customs, I knew a number of Customs agents and they were hiring at an even higher pay.

So I went to work with the Customs Service, and then in 1972 President Richard Nixon came in and decided that there'd be one drug agency. So all those people that had been doing drug investigative work for the U.S. Customs Service would be drafted into the service of the Drug Enforcement Administration, which Nixon created. I went along in the sense that my hours with Customs had been predominately in the drug-enforcement field, so they cashiered me, if you will, out of Customs and into the Drug Enforcement Administration.

I guess on the outside it would have appeared that there was a large effort. On the inside that meant that drugs were going to take on a political tilt. It was going to be a political football that would be trotted out when appropriate and the people of America would hear from their politicians that a great effort was being carried out, and that great effort that was being carried out was equivalent to a war effort because the president said it was so. That's what it looked like on the outside. On the inside, not a hell of a lot changed.

"WHO YA GONNA CALL?"

What put Miami on the map in the drug scene was the Miami lawyers. These guys made frequent-flyer mileage a daily word long before anybody heard of frequent-flyer programs.

You knew about traffickers arrested in New York City or New Jersey by their attorneys. If you made an arrest in Chattanooga, Tenn., and it was 10 kilos or 15 kilos of

TOM CASH

cocaine, you'd wait and see what lawyer showed up. If the lawyer came out of Miami, you knew you had a heavy trafficker. They came highly recommended and most frequently highly paid by the organizer or the trafficker who was headquartered in Miami. So it was the lawyer who telegraphed the message to law enforcement.

The reputation that had been gained by these attorneys was as very experienced; in fact, in the 1980-to-1985 period, the lawyers in Miami were far more experienced than the prosecutors in the rest of the United States in the drug trafficking. Prosecutors in places where I worked like Columbia, S.C., or in Nashville, Tenn., had no idea how to handle a drug-trafficking case and a good sharp lawyer with 15 drug cases under his belt from Miami would eat him for lunch.

"DON'T ASK, WON'T TELL"

Of course, here in Miami we were certainly right on track. We had the spectacle in the '80s of Leonel Martinez, our Metro-Dade "Man of the Year." We can never forget Leonel. We named a street after Leonel. We gave him the keys to the city. He was a pillar of the community, Latin Builders Association, and so forth. He was owner of a $3 or $4 million home in Cocoplum, which was known to the agents as Cocaineplum after all the cocaine traffickers that moved out there and built these enormous homes.

We had accepted that there were people who were miraculously successful and miraculously wealthy and let's not ask too much about them. After all, one of the things we do know is that money buys legitimacy, and when these people were coming out of Biscayne Babies and spending money freely from Porsches to yachts, it was very rude to ask them where they got their money.

A PLAN OF ACTION

Miami was the focus of our investigative efforts during my tour in Washington, just before coming to Miami. I personally added 53 new agent positions that we had received from Congress to the office in Miami, because Miami had shown again and again that the amounts of money that were involved clearly indicated that it was a leading area of that time. During the time I was a special agent in charge in Miami there were hundreds of millions of dollars seized every year from drug traffickers. I'm talking about between $150 and $300 million a year.

Miami was in the height of its activity. The tide was beginning to change. Additional prosecutors were being considered. Things were changing. Carlos Lehder had just been brought back. He had been extradited from Colombia. He was to be the first, last, and only member of the Medellín cartel ever extradited to the United States.

Indeed the pressure was now on, because it was one thing to read a CIA top-secret report about who was a drug trafficker and who was not and what all that meant, and it was quite another thing to now prove beyond a reasonable doubt in a court of law in the United States, in a system that is geared with a basic premise of better all the guilty go free than one innocent man be falsely convicted. So this was a monumental undertaking to take on the Medellín cartel —and, for a change, we were in their face.

When I came to Miami the first thing I instituted was operational plans. I was told by many of my assistant special agents in charge . . . they didn't need operational plans. I said when we walked out the door, we were going to know what we were doing, where we were going, who we were going to see, who we were going to arrest. We also wanted to know where the closest hospital was, and I wanted it driven to and not just referenced

TOM CASH

on a map. So we changed our operational plan and I said there would be no raids on Friday nights, no raids on Saturday nights.

For the most part, we were not doing operations in the parking lot of a McDonald's near a playground; we were not doing arrests in the Dadeland Mall, in the parking lot of Dadeland Mall. If we could avoid it, we wanted to stay out of those areas where if it did go bad, it might go bad not just for the agent, but for innocent civilians as well.

THE BATTLE IS JOINED

In the communities of Miami there was great interest. The Cuban 100, the Miami Coalition, the Non-Group had an enormous impact. People that come to mind are Aaron Podhurst, David Weaver, Dorothy Weaver, Peggy Sapp from Informed Families of Dade County, Frederica Wilson. Innumerable people who stood up and said, *"No mas. No mas."* When all of that began to come into play, I was there at the first meeting when the Non-Group created the Miami Coalition and went to the Chamber of Commerce and made a statement of support of—my God, a term that was never heard of before—a drug-free workplace. Whoever heard of the term a drug-free workplace?

There's a big sign in front of this brand new Home Depot advertising help wanted. It advertises flexible hours, high benefits, weekends and weekdays schedules, but at the bottom of this sign, in very high red letters, was the statement: "However, if you have ever used drugs you need not bother to apply." That's a message. That's how you turn it around.

JEFF LEEN

Jeff Leen is a Herald *investigative reporter.*

BY
JO WERNE

Shelley Kravitz

Shelley Kravitz is a Dade County Court judge. She was elected without opposition in 1992. Actually, finding a robe that fit was the hard part.

I grew up in South Hialeah on a street called To-To-Lo-Chee Drive. All of our streets had Seminole names. It was a great street to live on. It had beautiful palm trees, before they were wiped out by the blight several years ago. It was the kind of street that children could actually go out and play. We had a very close neighborhood. It was in the Deer Park section of Hialeah, which is in Southeast Hialeah, where deers actually roamed.

It was a wonderful little neighborhood. At that time the city of Hialeah had a population of about 50,000 people.... We used to have cow pastures. My parents, when they first moved to Hialeah, would be killing snakes all the time. That's how isolated the area was. When I was in about the third or fourth grade that's when we started experiencing the Cuban immigration. It seemed that most of the Cubans centralized themselves in Hialeah.

My father has always been an adventurous sort. When he got out of the service, he went to college and went to law school. He was on the G.I. Bill and he came to Hialeah and he thought, "This is a place that is up and coming, and I see a lot of room for growth and I want to grow with it." So he chose to raise his family there and to this day he still practices law in Hialeah.... The Hialeah/Miami Springs area was not an area where there were many Jewish families living.

[In the '50s] in Hialeah, there was a club called the Sportsman Club. It was on West Fourth Avenue near 49th Street and it's where the KKK met. Jay Morton, who was then the owner and publisher of the *Hialeah Home News,* went to investigate it and wrote a big exposé about the club and because of that he was shot in the leg. It was a very tumultuous time. In Northwest Dade there were no synagogues or Jewish community centers.

In my elementary school years, it was a very

SHELLEY KRAVITZ

idyllic time. We had a very close neighborhood. We had a fun club named after the street.

We had a pact that every single day we would do a different activity together whether it be going swimming at the Miami Springs Villa or play baseball or go to Greynolds Park. We had a close-knit neighborhood and it was a safe neighborhood. To this day my closest friends are my neighbors who I grew up with. There was something special about that neighborhood. In that little two-block area we had Justice Joseph Boyd, who [was] a Florida Supreme Court Justice, we had Ken Mattingly, one of the first astronauts to go to the moon. We had Circuit Court Judge Frank Knuck. We had Helene Kostyra, [one of the first] female troopers in the state of Florida, Rocky Lyons, who owns [a popular] hair salon. Leslie Armstrong, who has a radio show here called "Clean and Sober."

ANOTHER REALITY

It was when I went to junior high school—I went to Miami Springs High—when I first started to experience anti-Semitism. I didn't realize that I was that different until people started saying, "Well, how come you don't go to the local Southern Baptist church or the Catholic church?" When friends, or people that I thought were friends, found out that I was Jewish, they quit associating with me. People used to ask me if I had horns. They asked me why I killed Christ and I couldn't understand it.

I remember one day after school talking to my parents, actually crying to my parents, and saying, "Can I please move to Tennessee with my grandparents?" because they lived in a very small Jewish community and it was close-knit and I felt I would be protected there. I remember my father saying, "This is life. You better get used to it. You're Jewish and you can't run away from it." I think that really strengthened me.

When I was in high school, and because I wasn't accepted because I was Jewish, I started hanging out with more of the nonconformist group. I guess it was the hippie generation, and I remember it wasn't cool to do real well in school. So I could never tell any of my friends how well I was doing. One day I was mortified when the principal got on the PA system and mentioned to everyone that I was just inducted into the National Honor Society and was a National Merit Scholar. I was so embarrassed. My friends felt I was a traitor. At that time there were very few students from Miami Springs High who went away to college.

What's interesting is that because I'd grown up with so few Jews, when I went to Emory University I had never heard the term "JAP" before—Jewish American Princess. When I heard a woman referred to as a JAP, I thought, "Well, is she Asian?" I truly hadn't heard that term. That's how isolated I was from other Jewish friends. That's when I started getting more involved in Jewish activities and finding out more about my heritage.

YET ANOTHER REALITY

I wound up going to Emory University in Atlanta, Ga., my first year. I realized that there wasn't enough there to offer me. Everybody there wanted to be a doctor or a lawyer, and at that time I didn't know what I wanted to be. I just knew I wanted to be a community activist. I wanted to go to a school that could provide me with more of a liberal education, so I transferred to Antioch College, which is in Yellow Springs, Ohio. It's a work-study school. It really opened my eyes, because every other semester you would get a job working in different places. I wound up teaching in an inner-city school in Atlanta, teaching in a very wealthy

SHELLEY KRAVITZ

school in California, then teaching in a free school in the city of San Francisco itself where the students were from 4 to 14, and they were all mixed in in the same class. It was very interesting to see that interaction.... It was definitely an experimental school.

When I came back home I taught for several years in Dade County. I taught second, third, fourth, and gifted.... My father had been suggesting for years that I should be a lawyer, that I could do so much good. But he was a lawyer and I didn't want to look like I was copying him. We liked to lock horns. We are very much alike. I decided, "I want to be an international lawyer and I want to help poor people here and abroad." I moved back to Hialeah. I practiced law with my father for 10 years. I graduated from the University of Miami [law school] in 1982 and practiced with my father.

After many years of practicing I decided, well, it just makes sense for the next step for me to go for a judgeship. That's when I ran for judge. That was 1992.

It was interesting because I have long blond hair, I'm on the petite side, I'm only five feet, and I guess I look younger than my years. When I was running, people couldn't believe I was at that time 38 years old. People would say, "You can't run for judge, you have long hair. You look too feminine. That's not what a judge looks like."

I decided I'm going to be who I am. Everything worked out fine.

I could never find [a judge's robe] to fit me. It was very difficult. So I had [to] roll up the sleeves and it was sent back to the company that made it three times. Finally I found one that fit OK and I just accepted it. My first day sitting on the bench was unique, because I went and sat in the chair and looked out over the courtroom. I was so low to the ground that I couldn't see above the lawyers in front of me. I couldn't see anyone in the courtroom and my first words that I uttered to the bailiff were, "Please get me a booster seat so I can see." Well, I tried a telephone book, but it was so slippery that I kept falling off it. It was embarrassing. I wound up standing up and nobody knew the difference—people stand up for the judge, so the judge stands up for the people.

JO WERNE

Jo Werne is the Herald's *home furnishings writer.*

BY
TOM FIEDLER

DANTE FASCELL

Dante Fascell served in the U.S. House of Representatives for 38 years.

Politics in Dade County has followed the change in populations. It's that simple. It may be an oversimplification, but it started out with the local gentry, the folks from Florida—like my wife's family, for example, seventh-generation Floridians—and all those folks who made up the so-called Crackers ran the town.

In those days, the sheriffs were the political powers in every county in Florida until the system was changed. So they ran everything. . . . D.C. Coleman was—when I first met him, he was state senator—before that, he was sheriff and he was the political center of Dade County in terms of authority and power and capability.

And then we started getting population movement coming from the North primarily and the old population was moved. But the significant political event that took place was the change, well, it was particularly noticeable on Miami Beach. For example, "No Jews allowed," that kind of thing. And with the migration of population coming from the North that soon changed.

I have no idea when that happened, but it certainly was before World War II. And the next thing was that you had a significant Jewish community that started then and still exists. But they had all the political power and they had the economic power in this community and they bought up all those old hotels on Miami Beach and changed them all around.

And so then the next political change that took place was the influx of the Cubans. . . . They have certainly taken over economically and politically in Dade County, no question about that. Which has brought a lot of changes in this county, both in economics and in politics.

The other influences, talking about national influences from other countries, Latin America, Asia, and whatnot, we've got all those, of course, but they're not as big as the

DANTE FASCELL

Cuban. So right now, I'd say it's not Latin, it's Cuban, although you got lots of other representation here.... So what is it, 80-something languages in our school system? Well, we're certainly a diverse community, but as far as the politics is concerned, I say the politics today is all Cuban and 40-50 years ago it was all Floridian, in that sense.

[The other changes] are the normal kind of development and economic things that go along with an increased population, which creates tremendous problems. So not just the Everglades, for example, or environment—the environment issues are not new in Florida—but there is a greater public awareness today than there was perhaps back when Marjory Stoneman Douglas wrote her book and tried to alert the American public.

But my first recollection on the environmental issue goes back to the dedication of the Everglades National Park, when John Pennekamp was editor of the *Miami Herald* and President Truman came down to dedicate the park. That was a big event, and it certainly made an impression on me. And one of the first things I worked on, of course, when I got to Congress was working with Spessard Holland to do something about settling the boundary question on the Everglades National Park.... The question was the northern boundary.

The original park boundaries were a lot greater than what was ultimately agreed to. It included all of Big Cypress. It included all of the Keys—and a compromise, in order to get the legislation fixing the boundaries of the park, we had to reach an agreement with the Collier people ... but obviously everything north of the [Tamiami] Trail was taken out as part of the agreement then. The Ten Thousand Islands were all given by the Colliers to the park.

And the other thing was that they moved the park boundary westward along the Keys so the Keys were not included. But perhaps, in retrospect, it might have been better to have done something else, but there was just no way to reach an agreement. The same way with the "hole in the doughnut," which was the major agricultural area in Homestead at the time. [It] allegedly produced five crops a year.

Because of the increase in population—[the] population pressure is so great, you know—but actually we've been out of fresh water for a long time. We're just drawing down on the aquifer, without any rationale as far as I can tell about what we are going to do in the future. I tried, oh I don't know, 25 years ago, to get the county commission interested in saltwater development with atomic energy, but we just never could get past the day-to-day thinking. We're gonna have a fresh-water problem if we just keep developing and we keep bringing people in and we don't do something about fresh water pretty soon. The aquifer is not going to supply the water we need.

And then, of course, we dug all those canals and had saltwater intrusion. I suppose we would have had saltwater intrusion regardless, but we dug the canals in good faith.... I got in a boat at Flagler Street and 12th Avenue and rode a motorboat all the way out to the middle of Hialeah to meet Bob Graham's father, Cap Graham. And, you know, we had to make a decision. It was either people or whatever and the decision was tried to protect the population as much as possible and that developed the whole Central and Southern Florida flood-control district, the largest project of its kind in the world.

And we are still learning as we go along 50 years later. We haven't. All of it was done in good faith. There was no malevolence about this at all. It was just that the engineers and situations—facts

DANTE FASCELL

emerged. Things changed. It's like learning about the course of water underground. I don't know why people thought levies would stop water and impound water. I can remember asking that question: "Why would the water be impounded because you've built something above the ground, when it goes underground and runs like a river?" I never got a satisfactory answer to that. But we built them anyway.

And so we learned as we went along. We're still learning. We're behind the curve, environmentally speaking, in Dade County. We're going to stay behind the curve. And Monroe County is the same way. We'll be lucky to save anything at all. It's a real uphill battle and the reason is very simple. I mean it's just people. You just can't, the land cannot take the people. So whether we go clean out into the Everglades and kill all of the trees, and the panthers, and the sawgrass, and fill in the muck and all that, it's still not going to satisfy the population demand.

And then we start going up. Well, how high up can you go and how thick can you make it? Well, it's pretty high and pretty thick right now, in my judgment. But, we're going to keep doing it and if we don't figure out some way to have some kind of balance, whereby man and nature can live in harmony—very difficult to do, where mankind is a natural destroyer and killer. So, whether or not you can get enough education out there and enough interest and support to preserve a little something, I'm afraid we're going to do just like some past civilizations, just destroy ourselves into nonexistence.

But I didn't mean to get philosophical or pessimistic—just trying to be realistic about where we are, and it's always an uphill fight, and I was privileged while I was in public office to join the uphill fight, so to speak. I just felt it was very important to put some interest and balance in the environmental aspect of our life down here.

TOM FIEDLER

Tom Fiedler is the Herald's *political editor.*

BY JOHN PANCAKE

XAVIER SUAREZ

Xavier Suarez, one of 14 siblings, was born in Cuba and raised in Washington, D.C. A two-term mayor of Miami, he came to the city wielding a Harvard law degree and a love of basketball.

I came to Miami in 1975. Miami was first of all cohesive. There were neighborhoods where you really could live and work and get your car repaired and go shopping and eat at night. The Little Havana neighborhood to me was utopia. I would have dinner at a little Chinese restaurant that was on 12th Avenue and Flagler Street. I remember that the special fried rice was $1.29 and I would have milk. I wasn't too schooled in the ways of the world in 1975.

There was obviously at the time, there was upward mobility. So a lot of people were moving out of Little Havana and were moving to the suburbs and buying the big houses, but there wasn't yet what you might call the "Cocoplum factor." There weren't that many people that were in a position to buy rather huge and expensive homes. It was mostly working-class and middle-class professionals that were struggling to make it. A lot of the Cuban doctors were ready, really, barely to practice. The lawyers were beginning to take the exam for the first time under a special program. I ended up studying with those fellows and it was interesting for me, culturally and historically, to become acquainted with the struggle of exiles who had not been assimilated and had not studied here and were given a special opportunity to become lawyers by studying two years at the University of Florida with great sacrifice.

So there were some inequities there that you could see, and yet there was a lot of networking. They were very fatherly and motherly towards us. They helped [me] out too, even though they recognized that [I] had a heck of a head start on the ability to practice law.

An interesting phenomenon happened. It's kind of a sociological thing. The American culture to a great extent glorifies young people. All world cultures don't do that. In the case of Cuba, if you were a

XAVIER SUAREZ

young whippersnapper, you know, 22 years old and right out of law school, people wouldn't necessarily listen to you all that much, because you just had to prove yourself.

Yet now that I had a degree and the degree was from Harvard—and apparently this was really, really important to people—if there was a conversation and a discussion, people would want my opinion.

Young people were beginning to be viewed as having something to offer, partly because we were bicultural and partly because we had begun to assimilate in a system that obviously has created the wealth and the political stability it has. There was beginning to be a respect for that.

You saw the beginning of an amalgam, I guess, of some of the best of the Cuban culture and some of the best of the U.S. way of doing things, especially in the political arena.

There was a lot of respect for the fact that, people were always wondering in Little Havana about the fact that American politicians could have big battles during an election and really insult each other and yet in the end they were shaking hands and sort of working together.

Particularly in the primaries, because at the end of the primaries the parties would sort of become cohesive again and candidates would say nice things about each other, after having insulted each other. That was a bit of an eye-opener and people were beginning to really realize that maybe that was part of the reason that Cuba had not had a democratic system. So I was immersed in all of that and really just quite taken by it.

ASSIMILATION POLITICS

One question I would always be asked right after I was elected in '85 was, "Do you feel more like an immigrant or an exile?" The thought at the time was that [City Commissioner] Joe Carollo, who was then on the commission, was more sort of the exile politician and I was more the immigrant politician. I was more assimilated. One time I remember saying, "Carollo likes to suggest that I am not as Cuban as he is and sometimes other people say, 'Well, Suarez has clear traits of his Cuban background and does have a lot of affinity for that culture.'" Certainly I was trying my best to speak Spanish well and so on, and I knew that was an important part of the whole equation. One time I said, "I'm a better Cuban and I'm also a better American than Carollo. I bet you I know more history of Cuba than he does, and I know the Spanish language better and I certainly feel that I know the English better than he does and history and relate to it."

I cry when I hear the National Anthem, and I also get really, really emotional when I hear the Cuban national anthem. One doesn't detract from the other. The same in [both] languages. You don't detract from the English language because you happen to know Spanish or French or Greek or Latin. You actually enrich it. You don't detract from the American culture, whatever that may be, because you have other values or other cultural traits that are a part of you.

They are not in opposition. A lot of times, they are just in addition to one another.

I ended up having a funny situation in different elections. I had different affinities and identifications. I initially got elected with a high majority of non-Hispanic white votes, what we call here Anglo, which is a misnomer of course, and a high percentage of Hispanic votes, but Hispanics were never my highest. Later I had very good black votes and ultimately ended up in a situation... that I did a little bit better, in fact, sub-

XAVIER SUAREZ

stantially better, with non-Hispanic whites than I did with Hispanics. I don't know exactly what that reflects.

A LITTLE MORE EQUAL

The prior mayor was a very flamboyant and cosmopolitan vocal person who was accused of shooting from the hip. The fact of the matter is that he had pronouncements on almost everything.

To some extent I tried to follow a little bit of that. I tried to suggest that even though it was the weak mayor form of government, I tried to maintain the illusion that the mayor was really the chief policy maker. That got me into some trouble with my colleagues on the city commission, who felt left out. The fact of the matter is that if you try to be up front on issues and at the same time try to live within the law, which says you can't really consult your fellow commissioners without doing it publicly before a commission meeting, you would almost inevitably get into that problem.

You would announce some kind of initiative or propose some kind of a thing like a program or reform, and the commissioners would not have been consulted and they had equal legislative power. They had equal power. So they would feel a little bit miffed.

That happened to me for a couple of years. Some of my legislative programs got bogged down, but after a couple of years they seemed to realize that I had the bully pulpit—even though I didn't have any more power than they did.

JOHN PANCAKE

John Pancake is the Herald's state editor.

BY
OLGA CONNOR

JOSE ENRIQUE DAUZA

Jose Enrique Dauza, a Bay of Pigs veteran, still stands ready to fight.

I was born in Pinar del Rio, Cuba, on July 15, 1923. When I left Cuba and came to Miami, I was 37 years old. I had been conspiring against the Castro regime and was one of the key members of a clandestine organization called M.R.R.—*Movimiento de Recuperación Revolucionaria* [Revolutionary Recovery Movement].

I came to Miami on a regular commercial flight, using an exit permit I got from a person who worked with Fidel Castro. Up until that time, I had not been persecuted, even though our group [the M.R.R.] was very active and I had devoted myself almost entirely to it. The M.R.R. was the group that maintained the closest contact with the United States government, specifically with the Central Intelligence Agency.

I knew Castro personally and never liked him. The year I finished law school, he was entering law school and sought the job of president of the student body. Traditionally, the post went to a senior, so I supported the senior we all wanted as president. Castro lost the election.

Later, after I left law school, I established many connections with labor unions in Cuba and the consensus was that Castro's movement was infiltrated by Communists. That was about 1958.

It never occurred to me that I would be arrested. And I'm no superhero. But I felt so full of faith, so angry at what these people were trying to do, that I was eager to square off with them. My blood boiled.

[After the Bay of Pigs] my colleagues and I began to reorganize and see if we could do something else to fight Castro. In June 1961, we planned an operation in which we would sail to Cuba in a ship we already owned and we would fire upon the U.S. Navy base at Guantanamo Bay. Then the Americans at Guantanamo Bay would think they were being attacked by the Cubans and react against Castro. But one of

JOSE ENRIQUE DAUZA

the fellows spilled the plan and the FBI came around and arrested us.

I became an adventurer and a warrior because of my love for Cuba. When bombs started to go off in Miami (and I must tell you that I was never involved in that, I'm opposed to that) a reporter from the *Miami News* asked me how it was possible that Cubans might be involved in the bombings. I told him, "Friend, there are Cubans here who would be capable of blowing up the entire city if they had the explosives."

After that, in August 1961, the CIA recruited me to conduct operations on Cuba. I became a direct agent of the CIA. And I wasn't even an American citizen; I got my citizenship in 1972 or 1973. I'll tell you honestly: The only reason I became an American citizen was that having to travel overseas with a reentry permit was a devil of a nuisance.

I became an American citizen because, as a businessman, I had to travel overseas. If I can't go back to my country [Cuba], I'll remain an American citizen the rest of my life. This country helped us, despite the things that happened. Like the way they abandoned us in Playa Girón [the Bay of Pigs]. That's something I'll never accept.

I had been a CIA operative since August 1961, doing operations inside Cuba—about 100 of them. One time, during a raid...in Las Villas province, they shot me in the arm. At first, we conducted those raids thinking that they would lead to something. We felt that [then president John F.] Kennedy, after the Girón experience, wanted to do something definitive about Fidel Castro. A lot of our people went into Cuba to teach local dissidents how to operate, bringing them weapons and explosives.

We had about 500 or 600 people there. They're all still here, waiting. They're waiting to get the means, the resources to do something again.

If we exiles had the right kind of working arrangement with the U.S. government, we could do something; we've got plans. Not plans for an invasion. We believe the situation in Cuba has to be solved internally. But it cannot be solved internally without external aid.

We want our country to be truly independent. We are friends of the Americans but we're not collaborationists. We are not underlings.

If tomorrow the Americans gave me the means to fight again for my country, I'll seize the opportunity. I don't mind fighting alongside the United States. What I can't do is fight alongside communism. And who's going to help me? Only these people [the Americans].

Q: Did you ever become a lawyer here in the States?

No. I studied at the university [in] Gainesville and applied to the bar. But I passed only two out of three exams and struck out. My command of English is limited and in order to be a lawyer you have to be fluent in that language.

So a good job in real estate came up, with some gentlemen from Trinidad, and I became partner with them. I sold real estate to foreign buyers. I did well and retired.

OLGA CONNOR

Olga Connor is Viernes editor for El Nuevo Herald. *Renato Perez translated this interview.*

STAKING A CLAIM, MAKING A BUCK, STRIKING IT RICH

THE ART OF ENTERPRISE

HISTORIANS

Nancy Ancrum: Let's talk about enterprise; business, its institutions here.

Arva Moore Parks: Gotta start with Julia baby [Julia Tuttle], on that one . . . I am totally fascinated with this woman as a businesswoman. . . . When she made the deal with [Henry] Flagler, she gave him every other lot instead of a hunk of town. Now that to me is a very clever person.

And on the other side of the river, I think, Mary Brickell [has] started to get the due that is hers and not William, who was considered a bit of a loony-tune most of the time by everyone that talked about him. But these new Flagler letters I have, they're talking to Mary Brickell in 1896. . . . They're saying, you know. . . . go settle Mrs. Brickell down. . . . These letters between Flagler and his people down here. So, it's interesting to me that this great magnate of Standard Oil is down here dealing with these two women; one on each side of the river.

Dr. Paul George: I've just finished a history, or a biography, of the Burdine family and the stories —again, this whole frontier thing. War breaks out between the United States and Spain over Cuba, and there's a lot of soldiers down here, 7,500. William Burdine is in Bartow and business is so-so and he sends his son down here and he takes a covered wagon with all the supplies they had to set up shop to sell goods and supplies to soldiers down here. He writes back home and says "business is booming; I'm all sold out" and the Burdines decide to come down as a family. . . .

One of the oldest ongoing businesses in Miami, of course, is the Burdine business. And then, the self-taught nature of these people; they didn't go to Harvard Business School or Stanford. Roddey Burdine succeeds his dad in 1911 upon his death . . . and becomes one of the most talked about and followed merchants in America. . . . There were just pages and pages of newspaper accounts of his death. . . . because he was one of these unique human beings who was incredibly successful but didn't step on a bunch of people to get there.

Howard Kleinberg: Don't forget J.N. Lummus and Carl Fisher. They built something out of a swamp there. Consider again, as I was saying, in 1900 there were maybe two buildings on what we now know as Miami Beach. By the mid-'20s, it was America's playground.

Dorothy Fields: Like D.A. Dorsey—Dana Alba Dorsey— came in the late 1800s and settled in Overtown and was an independent carpenter, worked for Flagler when he wanted to. Evidently noticed Flagler buying land and providing housing for workers and he decided to do the same thing and did it on a much smaller level but certainly did it, to the point that he became the first black millionaire in Dade County. . . .

[His daughter has] talked about how he collected his rents in Dade and in Broward County in a chauf-

HISTORIANS

feur-driven limousine. I had heard that before. I thought it was because he was being brash, but it was because, she said, he had cancer and he didn't drive....

And each time they went to Broward County they would pull him over because of this black sitting in the back with a white chauffeur, I guess. I don't know if the chauffeur was black or white. ... Finally, she said after that was done several times, the next time he went he took his tax receipts with him and just put them on the table when they actually arrested him to show how much land he owned, which was quite impressive, and she said from then on, whenever they got to Broward County they had an escort, a police escort.

Nancy Ancrum: Dr. Clark, can you talk about the ease or the difficulty of exiled Cubans, professionals, merchants who fled Castro's Cuba in setting up their same enterprises here in Miami?

Dr. Juan Clark: Well, as you know they fled the totalitarian system and I would say that what happened was that precisely those who had greater initiative, in my opinion, regardless of the socio-economic level of the person—in other words, whether he was a lawyer or entrepreneur or perhaps simply had a small business or what have you ... especially after the Bay of Pigs and the missile crisis they began to think about rebuilding their lives here. In most cases, they brought only their talents.... So, it was a real struggle from the bottom in most cases. I remember, for instance, people that I know very well in my family, etc., they began packing tomatoes in Homestead and they had been entrepreneurs. Gradually they began to climb....

I think there has been a fairly successful story that I think is one that has to thank a lot of course the community here that opened arms and hearts....

But, again, I think, we also have to say that, not only the Catholic Church, but the Cuban Refugee Program was a great source of help there. It was, by the way, a sort of unique program, in terms of its length in the history of this country.... I think that they have repaid, by and large, you know, with their taxes and so forth, what was invested there, which was over a billion dollars.

Dorothy Fields: I wonder what Overtown would be like, if in fact the expressways, highways that were purposely put in, that divided the community, where we had entrepreneurs, people who in fact had businesses, had very successful businesses, primarily because of laws that contained them. They went ahead and built, they were beginning to build empires in some instances. I wonder just what those communities, especially Overtown, would be like today, if in fact the government had not come in and the business people who encouraged it and just disrupted them. I just wonder.

BY
TED REED

EDWIN STEPHAN

He didn't miss the boat, did he?

I was a Korean War vet and gave up my commission, came down to Florida for a vacation and ended up needing some money on a GI Bill. I went to Lindsey Hopkins here locally, to their hotel training, took courses there and, amazingly enough, in the middle of the course, the instructor passed away.

So they got me permission from, I think it was Tallahassee—a temporary certificate. So I taught the course at the same time, and had two jobs for a while. I was teaching school five days a week, and bell captain on Miami Beach for seven days a week. This should have been 1954—'54 and '55.

I worked at basically the Biscayne Terrace Hotel.... First I worked at, actually, the Casablanca, the Casablanca Hotel on 63rd Street. And that was a very swinging hotel at that time.

They had some labor problems at that time . . . I didn't even know about it, but I was hired immediately for the bell captain's job—and that probably paid 20 times as much as the school job.

Well, from that hotel I decided I wanted to continue in something else other than the bell captain's job, so I started at Biscayne Terrace in downtown Miami and took the comptroller's job. . . . I became then the president of that hotel.

We had some principals by the name of Keith Roberts and Stan McDonald who asked me if I was interested in looking into working for a cruise line because they were thinking of big things for the future.

The cruise lines, historically, down here had been pioneered by Mr. Lewis Frazier [Sr.], and he had the older ships. Some of them initially weren't even air-conditioned. There was the *Yarmouth*, the *Evangeline*, the *Bahama Star*, the *Orion* and the *Ariadne*.

We had the *Yarmouth* and then later we had a ship, the *Evangeline*, which became the *Yarmouth*

EDWIN STEPHAN

Castle, and that was going along well, but they had a disaster at sea.

The ship caught fire very rapidly; sunk off of the Bahamas. We had 400 and some people, and 90 didn't make it.

That was, basically it was the end of *Yarmouth*.

At that stage of the game, of course, there were a lot of American lines still in existence, basically running out of New York, and they came down to the Caribbean for the winter season, and we had a lot of them, as I said, that today aren't in existence. They were old established cruise lines that basically were in a different era. Fine ships . . . basically transatlantic, but then they came back in the winter and came to the Caribbean.

When I first came in here after '62, the *Queen Mary* and *Queen Elizabeth*, believe it or not, those gigantic ships, were making five-day cruises in this part of the Caribbean.

But this was an era that you could see was coming to a close because they could not compete. . . . The jet was running them out of business, and they had the old theory of various class passengers.

I went down to Rio de Janeiro and I picked up a vessel called the *Princessa Leopoldina*. It was a new ship. It only was five years old, Portuguese crew. We made a brochure on a weekend. I remember we were all up, had the kid next door make a picture for the front cover, had it to the printer Monday morning and two days later we had all our brochures out.

In two weeks, we had sold out the entire summer for the vessel. Carnival and Rio style ship. Very, very popular.

From there I started a line called Commodore Cruise Lines. We incorporated in 1968.

We were over at the old port, sitting in offices over there that, compared to today, would be unbelievable. I mean, it was all windows, just had air conditioning units in them. I was fortunate enough that I had the yacht basin where they put in these famous yachts. There was one . . . where Onassis used to dock there . . . so I had a really picturesque office over there.

FLOATING ROYAL CARIBBEAN

I really was anxious to get safe, new, modern ships, and especially some of the incidents that happened in the area that I felt very strongly about, so I wasn't pushing so much to be an owner. Ted [Arison] went out and found partners and . . . did it probably correctly.

I went out and found investors for it, and so some people said, "Oh, you didn't have faith in the cruise business." And no, it wasn't that. At the time I really was very anxious to come over sincere and not say, "I'm pushing my own wagon." I really wanted to get the new ships.

I think we signed our orders for the three ships in 1968. The first one, as I said, came in in November of 1970.

It's a period of transition, and it's a volume economy that you have to bring to the average American passenger and this is the way to go.

On the *Song of Norway*, we actually turned down all group business. The strange thing about it is that when you get a group, you usually get a discount because of the size of the group. But we turned it down on the basis that it doesn't matter if you don't get a discount or if you pay full rate. We still don't want a group. Of course, it used to drive travel agents nuts. They used to say, "Why?" I would try to go through it, and they didn't understand.

If a group canceled at the last minute, for whatever reason, that threw a monkey wrench into our machinery. Today if you tell anybody that, they say, "My God, how could you have been so independent?"

EDWIN STEPHAN

Well, we had the ships and we were filling them. They were doing well.

We didn't discount for several years and probably up to 75 percent of our passengers for all three ships were from California. They took advantage of the jumbo jets. We chartered aircraft and we sailed out of Miami.

Every week we have a one-week cruise, that's the *Song of Norway*, and a two-week cruise, alternating *Nordic Prince* and *Sun Viking*.

We finally took two of our ships, *Song of Norway* and *Nordic Prince*, and built a center section for them in Helsinki. It was a 40-foot section. We split them in half and put in the middle the center section and now the ships were 1,000-passenger ships instead of 700.

The passengers had more square footage per passenger inside and outside—and that was on the sun decks and the interior—than they had before. We didn't need more engines or more galleys or what have you, so this worked out real well, 1978 and 1979.

Never split the *Sun Viking*. That today is still the original 700. But we just sold the *Nordic Prince*. . . . We sold it for $55 million. That was more than all three ships cost originally.

TED REED

Ted Reed covers aviation and cruise lines for the Herald.

THE WOMEN OF THE S&S

BY LARRY MEYER

Irma Gasser, Lois Cloutier, Yolanda Quiñones, and Karin Rippberger dish it out—with attitude. They have to—they work for Charlie and Jeanne Cavalaris at the S&S Restauant.

Karin Rippberger: Well, when I first came to Miami in 1976, I had to get a job. The easiest one was being a waitress. I came from Germany, I didn't have college, so I started as a waitress. Then one Sunday morning Lois called me up. She said, "Come on down, I have a job for you." And that was 11 years ago. I have been here ever since. Charlie never thought I was going to make it; he threw me out every day. "You are too soft! You can't make it here! Speak up!"

Lois Cloutier: And then he saw that you were not so soft as he thought you were. She has a big German temper, and when she says no, she means no.

Karin: I am so used to the customers, a lot of times I say, this is it, I am not coming back the next day. Some days we have bad days.

Yolanda Quiñones: I was born in Ponce, Puerto Rico, and came to the United States when I was 2 months old and lived in New York for almost 30 years, left New York, and came to Miami, and have been working with Charlie for 13 years. My customers know me as "Puerto Rico." That's the nickname they gave me. Sometimes I am out in the streets, in the mall, shopping, and I hear a voice "Puerto Rico, Puerto Rico." I know it's me, so I turn around and sure enough it's one of my customers. So wherever I go, there's someone there that knows me.

Lois: I came here in 1953. I worked for several years on two jobs. The last one was 14 years with Charlie Cavalaris. They call me "the Warden" because when Yolanda came there, she thought I was bossy. She gave me the name, and it's stuck with me ever since.

Q: On a typical day, the S&S always seems busy. Is it always?

Yolanda: Every day is a new adventure at the S&S, every day. I come in at 1:15, I relieve Karin. Karin goes home and I take over.

Irma Gasser: I [serve] seven stools.

THE WOMEN OF THE S&S

Lois: [Karin's customers] sit there, holds hands with her. They are all crazy about her. They like to sit with the German blondes. Me, I am the warden, I am rough, so I get the newspaper people.

Karin: I am just nice, and they take it the wrong way, that's all there is. Everybody has their own idea. I am just nice to the customers. I don't see nothing wrong with that. I am single.

Lois: All the older men like her.

Yolanda: I have a lot of customers that work in the arts on 36th Street—hairdressers, waiters, bartenders. I have several judges that I am crazy about, you know, as customers. They make my day. I look forward to seeing them. I have lawyers and I also look forward to seeing them too. I have policemen; I like policemen. My son is a policeman, and I seem to have something that attracts them as a waitress.

I enjoy them and I try to give them good and fast service because many times they get a call and have to leave their food. Sometimes they come back an hour later—Charlie holds their food for them.

I have been waiting on [lawyer Ellis Rubin] for many, many years. With Ellis I know exactly what he's going to eat. He doesn't have to tell me. Mr. Rubin loves fish, he loves his fish, his french fries—which he shouldn't have.

Irma: Mostly older couples come in my station. I know right away what they want—salad or iced tea first, or soup. . . .

Everybody is like family. I know their business, their lives, they are like family. If you are not there one day, [we wonder] what happened, why aren't you there.

Lois: It's easier for us—when we see them coming—to have someone get the order in the kitchen before they even get in.

Yolanda: Well, I have certain customers that I tell, "I will give you $2 to go someplace else." They are picky, picky, picky. You know that if they run out of butter they are going to complain, if there is no whole wheat they are going to complain. So as you see them come in and they are ready to sit down, you tell them, "Listen, I will give you $2 to sit in somebody's station" because you don't want to hear it. Let me tell you—they laugh because they know that they are picky and sometimes we ran out of stuff. So before they sit down you let them know that there is something missing and if you are going to give me a hard time, go sit someplace else.

For instance, my judge—he gets a kick out of it. Before he sits down, I have his water with his lemon, his salad, and a cup of soup—he likes a salad and soup every day. And he loves it, they love that attention. They all love that attention, they really do. [Another customer] loves it because he's single. He's in his 60s, and he really loves this attention. A lot of them come because of the attention we give them.

Lois: I know certain people that don't particularly like to sit with me. Maybe some people don't like big women. If you get up and see a pretty, little girl looking at you, somebody that's nice looking, they feel better sitting with her.

Yolanda: You know, the people from the arts are good tippers because they make a living out of tips. Some say they have and some say they don't have. When it's my birthday, they'll bring me a little flower or they bring me a pin. It's not the value of it, it's just the thought of it that says they remembered.

Lois: Karin has a man that brings her orchids off his orchid tree every morning.

Q: This is one of the last places in the universe where you can get homemade mashed potatoes. Tell us about the menu.

Karin: Breakfast, we have two

THE WOMEN OF THE S&S

specials, we have the S&S special, that's scrambled eggs and chopped ham mixed together, and then they have the L&C special—it's Canadian bacon and two eggs, with cheese on top. Home-fried potatoes and grits, oatmeal, toast, and coffee.

Irma: Monday, we have beef stew, stuffed cabbage, and ham. The ham with applesauce or baked beans, stuffed cabbage. We have mostly mashed potatoes, carrots, string beans, cucumber, salad, homemade applesauce, and two vegetables; Tuesday, we have turkey, chopped steak or weiner schnitzel, hamburger, cheeseburger, anything you want.

Wednesday, we have the special meat loaf, and pot roast that comes with apple sauce and dressing and the meat loaf with two vegetables as well as the pot roast. On Thursday we have pot roast, which is special, and Friday we have salmon, snapper and shrimp creole. Everything comes with two vegetables. Saturday we have shrimp creole, special meat loaf, and homemade french fries. Then we have homemade pies, apple pie, cherry pie, pumpkin pie, and peach pie. Also homemade rice pudding. Everyone is crazy about the rice pudding—they want to know the recipe for the rice pudding.

Q: I have never noticed any of his food changing with the times. People say they have to eat lighter, less salt. Has Charlie changed the way he cooks?

Lois: Charlie says, "If you are sick, go to the hospital. Don't come here to eat."

LARRY MEYER

Larry Meyer is executive assistant to the publisher of the Herald.

Haydee and Sahara Scull

BY NORMA NIURKA

Beneath those skin-tight, polka-dot dresses beat the hearts of two women for whom life is an art form.

Haydee: We are professional artists, graduates of San Alejandro School in Havana, class of '52. I had the great pleasure of arriving at this wonderful city in 1969; my sister in 1973. We both arrived on the Freedom Flights. I came with my children, Elizabeth and Miguel.

The first building that dazzled me was at 600 Biscayne Blvd. [Freedom Tower], a beautiful structure that reminded me of the Giralda in Spain [12th century tower of the cathedral at Seville].

The people at welfare were insistent that I work as a baby-sitter or as an elevator operator, but I kept saying, "I'm an artist, I'm an artist."

They said: "Yes, but what else can you do? If everyone who came on the Freedom Flights said they are artists, no one would work. Let's see: Paint something!"

They gave me a pen and a sheet of paper and I hurriedly sketched a Havana street scene, showing a big *mulata* strolling along the Malecón. When they saw that, the welfare employees were dazzled and told me they themselves would buy any pictures I made. That's how my clientele started. I sold my first watercolors for $20 each.

When my sister came, the same thing happened.

Our sponsor, our cousin, lived in New York. He placed his home at our disposal, and provided schooling for the children. When I arrived at the airport, before changing to the New York-bound plane, I climbed on a bus. I went for a ride through Miami and Miami Beach. In Miami Beach, I was fascinated by Ocean Drive because I thought the stone wall was the Malecón. "This is where I must live," I said to myself.

I started to walk and almost fainted when I came across Española Way. "Did I arrive in Old Havana?" I asked myself. "I must phone my cousin." My cousin told me, "Everything is ready here [in New York] for you and

HAYDEE AND SAHARA SCULL

the children. You won't even have to work." But we told him, "*Hasta la vista*, baby!"

Ever since, we've been creating our artwork, thanks to the second chance Christ gave us in this marvelous city, to the music of the wave and the sound of the palm trees, the tropical breeze. We always paint by natural light, never artificial.

Sahara: Remember the problem with the buses?

Haydee: The buses wouldn't stop for us, because we were two women, with two children, carrying paintings. Because the buses wouldn't stop for me, I had to walk to nearby places; I didn't have money to hire a taxi. Luckily, I met a well-dressed man, with diamond-like eyes, handsome, who asked us: "Is this painting for sale? Who made it?" And my sister and I said, "We made it. We're the artists."

The handsome, well-dressed man gave me his card and said "Come to my office tomorrow and bring the painting." The following day, I went to his office. He was the Cuban Jew, Abel Holtz, a banker. He bought eight of my paintings and sponsored my first exhibition.... This was in 1970.

In 1952, we did our first painting. The topic was Havana and the picture captured its beauty, its joy of life, its music, its color, its flavor. Our work is based on our environment. At first, it was everyday life in Havana. After we were surrounded by wonderful, marvelous Miami, we started to create works that pictured Miami and Miami Beach. We viewed Lincoln Road as a botanical garden, with all its plants.

We also painted the lovely and peaceful Ocean Drive. Twenty-some years ago, it was tranquil, with the old people sitting outside the hotels, looking like doves. When they saw us walk by, they were so happy that they kissed our hands. Nobody bothered you; everything was peaceable. You didn't hear car horns, because there weren't that many cars.

Cubans would say, "Haydee, why don't you come live in the Southwest? This is the place for the good life." And I would smile, Mona Lisa-like, I would say, "Soon, soon." But I didn't want them to know that we were preparing a testimony about Cuba and Miami. We have brought these two cities together in our artworks.

When we came on the Freedom Flights, we discovered a new world, a new horizon that gave us everything we needed to develop the most unlikely ideas, like the bottom of the sea or the stratosphere. Our art is everything that's new. I think we're connected to the 21st century. The three-dimensional art you see is a result of our influence.

We have a lot of projects in mind. One is a series of life-size sculptures of famous movie stars sitting in old cars parked along Ocean Drive. We'll have the image of Marilyn Monroe in a pink car outside the Marlin Hotel on Collins Avenue. The first figure is outside the Park Central Hotel, sitting in a 1937 Nash: Humphrey Bogart, as he appeared in the movie *High Sierra*. Motorists who drive past looking for a parking spot usually stop because they think it's a driver about to pull out. Others stop for a closer look, because Bogart has a very sour expression on his face.

Sahara: Ever since we were 14, we designed our own clothing.

Haydee: ... and the modistes in Havana were startled, because they were such daring designs. For example, a triangle-shaped opening at the back, just over the tailbone, showing the skin. Our shape is not standard; we're broader than we're tall. We're size 12 from the waist up and size 40 from the waist down. So, we decided to make our own clothes and our styles are very personal.

We try to dress like the *vedettes* [nightclub dancers] of the 1950s,

HAYDEE AND SAHARA SCULL

who had big hips. Here in Miami Beach, you can wear anything you want, and people will applaud you. No complexes.

We have a surfeit of love. It's divided between God, our art, and our large family. We are grandmothers. We love our art and are always busy. That's why we think we're immortal.

Sahara: I must tell you that we've been chaste since 1970.

Haydee: We have found happiness and are always full of hope, of faith, because we know the future will be better than ever.

[Miami's] so close to perfection that it scares us. The city of Miami resembles us, because of its joy of living, its generosity, its spectacles, its major events, like the Summit, the Super Bowl. The Arts Center is going to be very beautiful.

Maybe we ought to change our names. Instead of Haydee and Sahara, we should call ourselves Miami I and Miami II. My imagination may be running away from me, but I do think we're at the right place at the right time.

Sahara: Our life is like playtime.

Haydee: Twenty-five years ago, the Beach was tranquil, mellow; old people sat on the porches. Now, it's an explosion of color and life. People have to take to the streets, not to walk but to dance, to wiggle their waists, their hips. People need to enjoy themselves; everything must be done from that perspective.

Quietude may be nice, but it's more suitable to a hospital. We're always moving, searching for something unusual. We're not at ease; we don't believe we have succeeded. Incredible events are yet to come, events with movement, with life . . . and we're prepared.

NORMA NIURKA

Norma Niurka is the arts writer for El Nuevo Herald. *Renato Perez translated this interview.*

BY JACQUELINE CHARLES

JOENEL CEREMY

"You have no choice."

The first job, I was working in Miami Beach, in a hotel. I would vacuum the floor and fix the beds. They started me with $3 an hour. After that I get $3.75. I drove a truck making deliveries.

You look for a better job. When you find better, you wait until you see how you can manage your budget, how you can pay your bills, if the job has no opportunity like insurance coverage.

Sometimes you work some place and the boss tries to use you. They don't pay you enough money, and they want you to do more and more. If something like that happens, OK I'm not going to fight you. I quit, because I know I can find better job.

It's hard, because now there is only one check coming in. When [my wife] was here, there were two checks coming in. Now it's too hard for me. At least I'm not sick and if I pay the bills, I feel good. When I think about her my heart feels quite [sad] . . . but there is nothing I can do.

My dream is, I would like to get money to buy a trailer here. I need more money to live.

With any job, they sometimes see you working hard. You deserve a raise and then you expect to get a raise. They say, "Bad news, no raise." Then you don't feel too good. At the same time they say "bad news," they ask you to do more and more.

It's no problem for me. Myself, I can't complain. First I say thanks to God, because you get good health and you never get sick; sometimes you could catch a cold, but you always find a way to pay your bills. What you are looking for is to get good health and go to work and pay your bills.

You have no choice.

JACQUELINE CHARLES

Jacqueline Charles is a Herald Neighbors *reporter.*

BY
ARMANDO CORREA

TEO BABUN

Teo Babun, president of a development firm, has made the work ethic work for him.

I am 48 years old. I arrived from Cuba in 1961, at the age of 13. We came to a very different Miami from today's Miami. My last two years in high school were spent in St. Petersburg, at a naval academy. From there, I went to Michigan, where I studied electrical engineering and business. I got an MBA at Michigan Technological University, or Michigan Tech.

In 1978 I bought my own electrical products company. Then I became an entrepreneur. The company, Line Electric, was a traditional factory that had scaled down; I was managing my own company.... That company made me famous. I was Cuban, I was a Hispanic, I was in a business not usually operated by Hispanics.

My family was involved in the maritime shipping business in Cuba and took it up when they moved to the States.... After I moved to Miami [in 1987], we started other businesses.... We have Cuba-USA Ventures Enterprises, to create a $3 million fund to prepare for Cuba's reconstruction.

We also started Cuba-Caribbean Development Company, which conducts research on infrastructure and such, which helps American companies to make plans. When the time comes that these companies can go to Cuba, they can immediately begin to operate.

We have brought many Cubans to this company, people who came from Cuba beginning in 1980. Many of them speak no English but know a lot about industries in Cuba: about the mining, electrical industries, and others. They have not had a chance to work as entrepreneurs in the United States, and previously were forced to take jobs way below their skills. Now, they can work in their fields—cement production, maritime trades, mining—and display their knowledge and prepare themselves to work with companies that will go to Cuba in the future.

TEO BABUN

As a Cuban, I don't want to draw attention to negative things. When things look positive, everybody loves you; when they're negative, then you're on the losing team. That's the capitalist process. We Cubans have learned it in the United States and have learned it well. The risks are there but if you persevere, if you're capable and work hard, you can get loans, you can find the opportunities to get ahead and succeed. But you can't always control all factors. And the factors that lead to a loss are the saddest of all.

[An entrepreneur's] success is based on his ethics and in the manner in which he focuses on the important concerns, not the urgent concerns. These are two different things; urgent concerns are based on immediate needs. If you worry about urgent concerns, you move away from what's important. And what's important for every individual varies from person to person. In our case, the family is very important and we must keep it together, working in a protected, contented manner. Religion is also important to us.

Most important for us is our work ethic, which is based on our responsibilities and our attitude toward God. Also important is our relation with the community, not necessarily the Cuban community (although it is important) but the community in which we live: Miami. What can we contribute to the community so we can all have a better future? Also important are our employees and their families.

Those four or five considerations are to me important. And if the entrepreneur can focus on them and keep them in focus, he will get ahead. Those considerations attract the talented people that are needed and keep them happy and willing to work with you.

Way at the bottom of the list are money and growth. These will come naturally, once the entrepreneur focuses on the important considerations I mentioned earlier. Now, there are some things that you cannot control, that show up unexpectedly. Your competitor can do something you weren't expecting him to do. The market might fall. The interest rate might rise.

My grandparents came from Palestine to Santiago de Cuba in 1902 or 1903, along with several siblings, also Palestinians.

My father Teófilo went into industrial work in Cuba. That wasn't something Cubans usually did.... Our family became well-known in Cuba's eastern region and that helped them start up a shipping company. Eventually, the Babun shipping enterprise was the largest in Cuba, much larger than the state-owned merchant fleet.

When the Revolution occurred, my father helped the Revolution—a lot. But when seizures came about, he was tried in Havana and accused of having aided the previous [Batista] government. That was before Castro declared himself to be a Marxist-Leninist, but my father could tell which way the wind was blowing and he came to the United States.

When they left Cuba in 1960 they left everything behind, except for two small ships that were undergoing repairs outside Cuba. One was in Nassau and the other in the United States.

We sold the ships. With that money, my father started buying World War II-vintage ships. He brought them to the Miami River and used them as cargo vessels for shipments to the Dominican Republic and Haiti.

At that time, about 5,000 tons a year of cargo left the Miami River for South America. Today, the tonnage is almost two billion.... Today, there is talk of dredging the entire river to keep the waterways clear. The Miami River is the third largest port in Florida, when it comes to cargo tonnage.

When my father died in 1987

TEO BABUN

the city named a street after him, in recognition of his work: North River Drive is also known as Teófilo Babún Drive. My father is known not just for his entrepreneurial talent but also for his tremendous patriotism. Because he had once helped the government of Cuba, he became a bitter enemy of Fidel Castro.

In the early 1960s, he aided many Cubans who came to Miami. He bought five or six houses in North River Drive, and gave free housing to the newcomers for six or seven months, just long enough so they could get their bearings and find jobs. Meanwhile, they had a place to sleep.

Much is said about how the U.S. government helped Cubans, but it did so only in terms of food. Cubans had to help each other. That was the exile community's greatest achievement, I believe. They helped each other to fit into U. S. life, into Dade County life.

During the Revolution, almost all of the trucks Castro used on the Sierra Maestra were donated by the Babuns and almost all the weapons Castro received came aboard Babun ships, which my father made available to Fidel Castro. Later, it was just the opposite. My father participated in practically every antirevolutionary action there was, from here and from other places.

For several reasons, I was never involved in that activity. But I did try to contribute to the process of anticommunism. Now that the Soviet Union has been defeated, my mission is to be ready for the Great Reconstruction that will take place in Cuba, and to help others get ready.

Armando Correa

Armando Correa is a reporter for El Nuevo Herald. *Renato Perez translated this interview.*

BY TONY PROSCIO

Reverend Dennis Tarr

"Jesus was one of the best marketers in the business," says Rev. Dennis Tarr, pastor of First Presbyterian Church of Miami on Brickell Avenue. "He told stories. He was real."

Usually in doing seminars around the country, which I have done for many years, in marketing, to institutions like Fortune 500 companies and start-up companies, I usually talk about the seven P's of marketing [planning, product, price, place, promotion, people, performance] but there are eight P's when it comes to the church, because there is another dimension [prayer]. Not that it can't be used in business. Some very successful businesses do use this eighth P, but it is usually not thought of in those terms.

[In 1988] this was a church in grave danger of ceasing to exist. The church had been up for sale for about 10 years, actually about eight years, for then a tidy sum of $27 million. . . . Being on the bay, I mean it's a terrific property, but the church was up for sale. And it represented not a forward vision of what the church could do with that money at all, so much [as] a desperate, last effort to leave the city, because the population for the most part had left.

The congregation had dwindled from its peak in 1957—then about 1,300 or 1,400 members. Packed services. People lined up. No place to park. That was the height of mainline church attendance in American history. The Eisenhower years. Postwar years of tremendous confidence in the American Dream, that we had won the war.

Mainline denominations reflect a balance of theology between personal salvation and social concern, a very healthy balance. You can't receive the gift of salvation without sharing very tangible things [with] your neighbor in need. I still think that is the energy that drives the best of Christianity, where, as Jesus said, you can't love your neighbor, unless you love yourself. . . . So this church, not unlike other urban old churches, mainline churches, flourished.

A lot of things happened in the '60s, in the [Vietnam] war. All the student

REVEREND DENNIS TARR

revolutions, in the late '60s and early '70s, the questioning of any institution with "authority."

In Miami in particular, during the late '60s and early '70s, there was absolutely an abandonment of people and homes. If you looked down Brickell Avenue, it was Millionaires' Row when this church was moved from Third and Flagler to across the river and to the south of the banks of the Miami River, to this location. There were no high-rises. There was no commercial [development].

The Brickell family, which had the Brickell trading post from the late 1880s or maybe even a little [earlier] than that, traded with the Indians. Gradually this property has now become, I guess, the second international banking community in America. So when the church moved here these were homes, luxury homes. There were neighborhoods.

With the riots in Miami in the early '80s, there was just still a kind of [continuing] abandonment of the city. A lot has happened. The city fathers have done a great deal to concentrate, to bring people back into the city. All the improvements going on in downtown. The high-rises, the Bayfront Park efforts, and now the Center for the Performing Arts, the government complex, the People Mover, the Metrorail, and the whole infrastructure of the city now makes this location again a very viable one.

I was very much aware who was moving into the Brickell area, Brickell Key, Key Biscayne, South Beach, the Grove, the Roads, and the primary targets for this church's parish. And [I] started to preach a series of sermons on renaissance and hope and let's stay in this place. Let's pray that God uses this location as a place of hope to this community, and to help turn around attitudes about downtown, the role of the church in the heart of a business community. What should it be doing to renew its mission, to find a new mission and the strategy to reach out to serve real needs in the community?

The church decided to stay. It took about 18 months of careful planning, praying, and sharing a vision of the potential in this location, of a very unique ministry of trying to serve the business community, the cultural community and anyone who wants to come.

We have a seminary called the South Florida Center for Theological Studies. It trains men and women for the pastorate. There're about 60 students and 15 faculty members. It's taught in three languages: English, Spanish and Creole.

We have a language institute here . . . anywhere from 100 to 300 students, studying some eight or nine different languages. Spanish, English, French, German, Russian, Japanese, Portuguese, Italian.

We have a ministry of research and Bible translation, the International Bible Society is headquartered here. . . . For the first time in 40 years [there will be] a new translation of the Bible in Spanish. So between fax, computers, modems, and about every three months the scholars fly in from all over Latin America, they are preparing manuscripts and they are about to publish the New International version in Spanish of the whole Bible.

So who are we? We are less than 200 who come from 53 different countries. This congregation is not the monolithic, WASPish, blue-haired group of Presbyterians. These are people from every walk of life celebrating what Miami is becoming, a great international city. . . . That is part of this church's mission, not only as the oldest historic church in the city, but to reach out and relate to the business world. . . .

If you look at the demographics of what is happening in the downtown area, on Brickell Key between now and Christmas, there will be

REVEREND DENNIS TARR

640 new apartments. You can walk over the bridge to this church. We're the community church, we're the community meeting place and we're the cultural center for that community. As you go down Brickell, there are right now under construction three more big high-rises. A block and a half away on the Miami River . . . the tallest building in Miami is under construction. Two giant towers, condominiums. This whole area is beginning to change.

Location has an implication in terms of our local mission as well. . . . So what we have done recently is adopt the local elementary school. Southside Elementary School is the local school in our area. It's on 13th and a block west of Brickell. It is one of the oldest schools in the city. It was built in 1912—350 children, we've adopted all the grades there. We have a team of about 12 volunteers who go, some every day, some once a week, to tutor, to love those kids, to listen and to be friends. We need to buy some sneakers, some T-shirts and some people need food. So we become facilitators in that as we adopted them and expressed our love to the community. Seventy-six percent of all those kids are below the poverty line.

This church is poised to celebrate its 100th anniversary next April and to look strong towards a healthy future in the next century. I feel very privileged to be a part of that transition, of that challenge of saving it and restoring it and dreaming about it.

Tony Proscio

Tony Proscio is an associate editor of the Herald.

ALVINO MONK

BY SUSANA BARCIELA

Alvino Monk makes black business his business. He is the publisher of the Greater Miami Black Resource Guide.

[Coming to Miami from Chicago in 1986] my initial impression was—I had two separate impressions, actually. And one that it was a very cosmopolitan, international, culturally rich area, and the other one, from the black perspective, that Miami was about 30 years behind the rest of the country.

Now, I've come to have a better appreciation for black Miami, and to the extent that I realize that it is the Deep South, [I have come] to the conclusion that it is really a very progressive city based on where it was and where it is now.

[Marie Brown, wife of ophthalmologist Dr. John O. Brown] brought to our attention this directory that she had done in Miami in 1958 and it was a black business directory.... The total population of Miami in 1957 was 651,600 white and 106,100 nonwhites. And then you know in terms of the Negro population here, it says 64,947 blacks were here in 1957.

And so we just found this so interesting in terms of where we were now versus where we were then. Back then, Miami was segregated, so blacks had everything: They had their own hotels, they had their own auditoriums, they had their own theaters, their own hospitals, you know, the barber shops and everything that they needed was right there in their community.

And [black travel agents] were coming here in 1988 for their annual convention and [Mrs. Brown] asked if we would help her to reproduce this book for these people.... But I didn't know where the black businesses were. I didn't know where the black professionals were, and we were like floating around out here not being able to make that connection to our community— that cultural connection.

So we took on this project to update this register in 1988 and we went through the Miami-Dade Chamber of Commerce....

ALVINO MONK

We were able to get funds from the Super Bowl host committee. What came out of it was a visitors' guide to black Miami for the Super Bowl.

And a very unfortunate thing happened. We had the riot then. We had 55,000 of these directories that were printed up that were promoting black businesses, black culture, and so it was probably the only, and most positive, thing that happened during that period. They actually blocked off the black communities, Overtown and Liberty City.

The riot sensitized me to the need for the black community to participate in the tourism industry, which was the No. 1—and still is—industry in this town. And I was amazed that, one, the [Greater Miami Convention and Visitors Bureau] didn't have enough information on the black community and that, two, it was a segment of the community that they simply were not promoting to the visitors or to the conventioneers that came here. So my job was to go out and sell the black community, the black businesses in particular, on the advantages of being members of the bureau.

At that time in '89 I think the statistics said that there were over one million black visitors that came to Miami out of seven million or six and a half million. And that they spent approximately $1 billion. And that was basically my selling tool. . . . In my opinion, we were making a lot of progress and then the Nelson Mandela snub came along [followed by a 30-month black boycott].

1958 VERSUS 1995

It's a real dichotomy in one sense. And in the other sense it just shows how much progress we've made. On one hand, we had all of these black businesses here and now it appears as though they're not there anymore—but they are. They diversified; they've spread out all over the county and they're all different kinds.

We've got over 346 different categories [in the guide]. So you can find a black business that does anything. We thought that it showed progress on one hand.

On the other hand, it also showed what integration had done. Our people were not supporting our businesses anymore as a result of integration. Our businesses, once they started mainstreaming, then black folks just stopped patronizing them. They started patronizing the better stores. So we found that the businesses . . . were having serious problems just even surviving.

Most of the businesses of Ma and Pop, maybe over 95 percent of them, have not grown, have no plans for growth, and are just surviving on a day-to-day basis. There are others that want to grow and don't have access to the information or the resources or the financing that they need. Then you've got a group of professionals, doctors and lawyers and bankers and accountants that, for the most part, seem not to be connected to the community at all.

Statistics say that there are 400,000 people of African descent here in Miami and they spend upward of over $2 billion, but there are less than 10,000 black-owned businesses and they only gross $300 million, so . . . only 10 percent of what we earned is being spent in our own community, and that's not enough.

And then the other problem [is] that you have these different ethnic groups in the black community and that, you know, is something that I've always enjoyed. Miami is really very international as far as the black community is concerned. Of the 400,000 people, the Census Bureau says 200,000 are African Americans

ALVINO MONK

and 100,000 are Haitians and 100,000 are West Indians. They don't count the Afro Latins, and not only that, they're undercounting the West Indians and the Haitians.

But the point is that they do outnumber the African-American population when you combine the other ethnic groups of African descent. They outnumber us two to one and really they set the pace and determine the agenda, I think, for the future of black Miami.

The other objective goal of putting the book together was to bring all these groups together.... We say these are people of African descent and these are their businesses.

SUSANA BARCIELA

Susana Barciela is a Herald *business writer.*

BY JACQUI LOVE MARSHALL

ELLEN JOHNSON

As sexton at Lincoln Memorial Park, Ellen Johnson tends the black cemetery founded by her godfather, Kelsey Pharr, who was appointed U.S. ambassador to Liberia in 1943 by President Franklin D. Roosevelt.

I am the sexton of Lincoln Memorial Park. That's what managers that are licensed to manage a cemetery are called. Lincoln Memorial Park was started by my godfather, Kelsey Pharr, and when he passed in 1964 I became licensed and became the manager.

I had all of the business cards made up with just E. Johnson because I wouldn't want to antagonize the men customers. They used to always come in and say, with a business voice, "May I speak to Mr. Johnson?" And I would say, "Well, Mr. Johnson is not here right now, but I'm Miss Johnson. Could I help you?" And, we would solve the problem.

During and prior to '64, all businesses and establishments were segregated, and so this being the business that he started—he also started one of the first black funeral homes in Miami—he then proceeded to start a black cemetery for blacks.

It was called Pharr Funeral Home and it was on Northeast Second Avenue.... He was asked to disinter because there was a black burial ground, as they called it at that time, in Lemon City, and he was asked to disinter those bodies and he did, to Lincoln Memorial. Also, when Flagler brought the railroad down, the majority of blacks in the city of Miami were buried in the back of the cemetery where the railroad had to go through. [My godfather] was asked to disinter those bodies. He moved them into Lincoln because it was the only black cemetery at that time.

We have a lot of blacks that were interred there that were entrepreneurs.

Well-knownest one of all is possibly D.A. Dorsey. Everyone knows and heard that name because there is a street named after him, a school.

Mr. Henry E.S. Reeves, who was the founder of the *Miami Times*, was buried there. There are quite a few that are there that schools are named after, just like Dr. Pharr,

ELLEN JOHNSON

my godfather. There is Kelsey Pharr Elementary School on 46th Street and Arthur and Polly Mays from South Miami; there's Mays High School. There was no high school or school of higher learning in Homestead and Richmond Heights area. So they bought a used bread truck and they used to carry the children up to Carver and Booker T. [Washington] for the high school.

We have quite a few others; in fact, the late Rep. Gwen Cherry, who was the first black woman legislator from the state of Florida, she was interred there, and we have Julia Jenkins Baylor; she organized the Y-Club, which was the forerunner of the YWCA for black girls in Miami.

And Florence Gaskins—she was an entrepreneur too. She organized the local black junior Red Cross for black girls. And, there is Artemis Brown, the first black blacksmith in Miami.

Marie Roberts, she was the first known person in the South to receive the master of arts degree in human relations, and she organized an experimental class which was a pilot study for the program she formed at Booker T. Washington High School.

Also Samuel Johnson is buried there and his children. One of them was Judge John D. Johnson, one was a radiologist and daughters who were teachers. And so, most of the families that we have at Lincoln were pioneers in their fields.

That's why, when I became involved in Lincoln, not only becoming a sexton, but also learning and going to the conventions of the Cemetery Association.

I heard something that was very profound to me, that was a quote [from] Benjamin Franklin. Whenever he goes to a town for business or pleasure he always visits the cemetery first. Why? Because he said he would see how the living people and relatives of the departed loved ones were taken care of. That way he would have an idea of the reception he would get from the people.

I got to thinking about that. During my godfather's tenure—during the '30s and '40s and '50s when all of these [people] I have mentioned were interred at Lincoln, they were entrepreneurs and the black community was thriving. But, if you look today, 1995, the black communities of Dade County are not thriving. But, I, myself, have made a dedication to perpetuating and keeping the cemetery, the black cemetery, to honor the departed loved ones that have went before.

JACQUI LOVE MARSHALL

Jacqui Love Marshall is the Herald's vice president of human resources.

THE FRUITS OF DEEP ROOTS, A SENSE OF COMMUNITY

THRIVING ON OUR HERITAGE

HISTORIANS

Dr. Paul George: Howard and I were talking beforehand about the fact that so few people embrace us as their city for whatever reasons, different reasons. But I think of an early time when there seemed to be a much greater amount of pride in this place as their city. I think of some of the early residents even, actually through the '20s and '30s, where they had made the big move from, oftentimes, a small Southern town or a large Southern town, to Miami and it *became* their city.

Dr. Juan Clark: I have been asking my classes and the people that can be considered of nonforeign stock, which means [neither] one of their parents were born abroad. It's a minority in all my classes. So, it means, you know, that of course we have this transient new community, etc., and it takes time for people to develop pride....

But, I think that's something that is developed. I can see it with the younger generation that I relate to, with my sons, my nephews, etc., etc. They feel very much identified with Miami as their city and I feel that that's something that is growing in a very strong way in general within the Hispanic community, considering this home....

I consider this home myself. Yes, I would like to make a contribution [in Cuba], but I consider Miami home also. So I feel that gradually, at least within the Hispanic community, we have this growing sense of belonging here and I think that we are all in this boat and we need to make it sail....

And essentially it takes time. It's a process of assimilation, adaptation. It's a two-way avenue, by the way, a give and take. Certainly, the Miami of today cannot be the Miami of 50 years ago and I think what we have is a city now that has been enriched by all this different bloods and different cultures and different races....

Howard Kleinberg: When my immediate family sits down to dinner for a holiday or a Sunday barbecue, there are 22 of us. We are a community unto ourselves. I got here just in time.... I had the benefit of going to high school here. When I arrived I was a newcomer.

As the years have passed and as the demographics have changed, I'm suddenly "old Miami" to a degree and I have retained that sense of roots. What makes it important is that my family has stayed intact in the Miami area when so many have not. What also makes it important is those people that I went to high school with 45-some-odd years ago, we have remained friends, we have married each other, we get together all the time, sometimes to complain about what's happened to the town, sometimes to wonder why we did what we did to the town, sometimes to wonder what the town did to us, but always that we are together and we are part of this community....

We're still holding onto the flag.... We understand the changes. We don't like 'em all, but we live with them.... It's not the same town. We realize it cannot

HISTORIANS

ever be the same town. But the fact that we've been Miamians for a long, long time still makes us proud of the town.

Dorothy Fields: Well, our roots are here and we plan on staying, and for the first time we have an opportunity and a responsibility to be part of change.... There are people that we don't know who are African American. But we are hopefully beginning to understand the diaspora, that we are all cousins, that our cultures may be different, but that we have a commonality of ancestry.

Arva Moore Parks: I guess I feel very blessed in several ways because I grew up in this town, with a family that loved this town and taught me to love this town, loved its history. I was taught to love all kinds of people and that there was great, wonderful learning....

I've probably lived in the same place and lived in five different Miamis.... If you look at what we've done in only a hundred years.... I think the Cuban story, coming into this town ... what they have done in this town, to this town, for themselves, is an American history phenomenal story, I think. That happened here where we live....

The final thing is, we're alive. This city is alive. The only things that don't change are things that are dead.

Dorothy Fields: [Arva's] from a middle class family and so am I. When I was born, my mother, her two sisters and her four brothers were all college graduates living in Overtown. It was the first family, African-American, black family, to have as many as seven children finish high school, college, and return to Miami to work until retirement ... in Overtown, right across the railroad tracks.

So my point is that we were middle class too ... but because we were black we had to live in a certain area.... We talked about all the good things and that's fine, but we didn't talk about the things that happened to people. It's important when you are going to talk about mosquitoes, alligators, and the wind and the sun, you've got to talk about the lynchings and stuff that went on here as a part of the whole fabric of this....

We did not do it to ourselves ... because the way it seems is, oh, the Cubans did this and they came and whatever. The Cubans could all be white if they wanted to. They could just change their names, the Z's and the S's, to anything else.

But as much as I used Artra— we really believed that if we used a bleaching cream called Artra, which was the best, if we just changed the color of our skin, that you would love us. More than that we could be like you and everything would be all right—and I'm surprised there aren't more black dermatologists [laughter].... But that was the mentality because we were "whitewashed" to believe it....

Here we are moving into the 21st century, and with all the optimism that I have, will race still be the issue? Time will tell.

BY BOB KEARNEY

BOB KAUFMAN

Bob Kaufman teaches American history and coaches basketball at Miami Killian Senior High School, but he's a Miami High Stingaree for life.

I've been living down here now 51 years. I was born and raised down here. The center of school rivalry was the Orange Bowl. You knew from the time you were growing up where you were going to high school. So you knew who you were associated with before you got there. School rivalries were really the only games in town, besides the University of Miami.

Of course, the Orange Bowl was built for Miami High, to begin with. Miami High and Edison was always a tradition down here—anywhere from 30,000 to 40,000 in the Bowl. One side totally red and white. That was Thanksgiving night. Every year you just did it: You ate an early Thanksgiving dinner and you went to the Bowl. Those games were classics and my dad started taking me to the Orange Bowl in 1949, when I was 5.

The school rivalries back then were just so much more school rivalries and not like today, which are between race and ethnicity. It was strictly a school rivalry. You lived and died your school colors. You weren't embarrassed to sing your school song and things like that. These were big things, of course. The first time Edison beat Miami High, they took the goal post and marched it back to their school and they still have it there.

Today kids would call a cab, I'm sure.

BOB KEARNEY

Bob Kearney is a former Herald *sportswriter and public relations director for the Miami Dolphins. He now manages special* Herald *projects such as the Silver Knight Awards.*

BY
JOHN BARRY

DENISE WALLACE

Denise Wallace is an attorney with Steel, Hector & Davis for whom life in Coconut Grove has been a blessing and a curse.

When people ask, "Are you from Miami?" I say, "No, I'm from the Grove." I guess we always felt this clannishness about being from the Grove. I don't know whether it comes from the knowledge that we are one of the first groups of pioneers and that we are probably the only self-contained community still left in Miami. Overtown, which was another self-contained community, has dissipated so vastly that one cannot call it a community any longer.

A large part of our community centered around two institutions—school and church. Because my parents were educators, that thrust them into a role of community leaders, whether they liked it or not. Because my grandparents and my mother were active in the church—my mother has been either assistant Sunday school superintendent or Sunday school superintendent all of my life, and she's still Sunday school superintendent—I guess that gave them positions of authority based upon those two institutions.

My father had always been a very vocal and outspoken individual, so he had a much more visible community prominence than my mother did. He worked for the Episcopal Diocese in one of their Opportunity Industrialization Centers, which was, I guess, one of the offshoots of [Lyndon] Johnson's poverty programs. He was also the first black affirmative action officer for Eastern Airlines.

I left Miami in 1973 or 1974 for college. It was still the Grove. There were no lines of demarcation in the Grove. I came back in 1978 or '79, and there were still no lines of demarcation in the Grove. I came back again in 1981 and all of a sudden there was a South Grove and the West Grove, which is historically the Black Grove. However, the distinction in the Grove from what I can remember historically was there was the village, which was the

DENISE WALLACE

commercial center of the Grove, and the West Grove, [which] was referred to by people as "colored town."

However, when you ask those that are of African descent, the Grove simply means that section that was the oldest part of Coconut Grove, which was the West Grove. Everything else would be referred to as the village. Now we have all these artificial lines of demarcation. They tell me that I live in the West Grove.

I actually went to grad school in Vermont, and from there I went to law school. At that point my father had died, and my parents still owned property in the Grove that my grandparents owned. My father, basically, was managing all the property and everything. So I knew when I was graduating from law school, I was like, "I'm not going back." And my mother was saying, "Oh yeah, I'm praying for you to come back." I'd tell her, "Don't pray for me, don't pray for me."

So I'm back, basically because there was lots of family property that nobody was seeing after, that needed to be managed. It all sort of fell on me.

It was emotional, and it's still emotional. It was a very practical decision in some respects and a very difficult decision in others. It was not the Grove I grew up in. So it was not a Grove that I could feel comfortable being in and having my children walk the streets. It was not a Grove that I sometimes would feel comfortable being in, but yet coming back at this point and being a divorced parent and trying to start a second career, I was confronted with, "Well, I can live out in Kendall where my mom lives and not worry about things and pay an exorbitant amount of rent, or I can move up here where I have property that needs to be managed." So I moved back to the Grove. I'm still mixed about it. I live in the Grove now. I don't have to live in the Grove.

From a lot of practical aspects, it is a good place to live. It's just that the city has just practiced such benign neglect in focusing on remedies for an area that can be easily cured of its ills. It just leaves me wanting to say, "I'm out of here, too."

I think one thing that integration helped erode were the social structures. [When I was growing up] you had basically people that you could aspire to be like. If it were the mortician, well, the mortician always appeared to have steady income, because people were dying. If it were the teaching—God knows when I hear what my parents made as teachers, I [wonder] how could they exist and how could they raise a family off that. Yet they were supposed to have been authority figures and very well respected, so you had people aspiring to be like them. We had black property owners, we had, for all intents and purposes, the equivalent of black millionaires.

Then we had our regular bums who would see you places and would tell you, "You don't need to be here." I remember that when I was growing up there were four bars on every corner. I never went to one of those bars until I was in my late 20s. One of them sold food. They sold Chinese food, and you would go around the back door to get Chinese food. I remember I was a teenager, and one night coming home I was going to get some Chinese food. I went around back and someone looked at me and said, "Wallace, you know you're not supposed to be here." I said, "Oh no, they're going to tell my dad, and I'm going to get killed."

So you had those types of things and you were always getting encouragement from whom you would least expect it. There's a saying that most people who had respectable families—or even if

DENISE WALLACE

they didn't—once the streetlights come on you're supposed to be inside. Whether it came from a former schoolteacher or whether it came from a drunk, you had this being reinforced that you are not doing what your parents want you to do. A lot of that is missing now. . . . I see why people who have grown up in the Grove say they're not coming back.

The one reason why I'm vocal, and I guess why I feel so strongly is that I don't want to be remembered on a placard, "This is the home of the first Bahamian settlers." I don't want to be remembered on a 3 x 5 metal sign on Charles Avenue: "Pioneers of the early Black Grove." I don't want that as my legacy. I don't want a bus driving west and people pointing out a wooden shotgun house saying, "This is what remains of the Black Grove."

That is not how I was raised. That is not what I remember. I remember going to school, football games at Grand Avenue Park, and cheering on Carver. I also remember hearing gunshots behind the Tiki Club, but that was not an accepted practice. The crime that is existing now is being allowed to exist. It is not something that is wanted.

It's a neighborhood with a future that I am uncertain of. I guess in some small way I'm continuing to fight as much as I can without saying, "I can't take this anymore."

There are days that I wake up and say, "I don't have to deal with this. I don't have to manage this property." The IRS tells me that I have the financial wares, that I don't need to. If I feel that way—and I have a very undying commitment to the Grove—then I know others do. I don't know what can be done to avert the tides.

JOHN BARRY

John Barry is a reporter and columnist for the Herald's Living & Arts *section.*

BY PAT MAY

ROBERT LAMME

Robert Lamme, a former illustrator for the Miami Herald, *has seen a lot of history in the making.*

MIAMI'S NEW AIRPORT

Charles Lindbergh gave the dedication speech [at the airport's 1927 opening]. The main buildings were there; one of them was completed and the other, which was the administrative building, I guess, wasn't quite completed yet. And there was a partly finished hangar there.

After this dedication speech, [a] plane took off. Ed Musick was the pilot. And he flew a twin-engine amphibian down to Key West.

All the ceremonies took place near where that administration building was. I remember he was on a balcony they had there, Lindbergh was.

[My buddy] Harold Kantor and I were coming into the place. Before we got to where all the speeches were going on, there was a guy there, parachute jumper, packing his parachute. He was going to make a drop from about 10,000 feet and wait until he was almost to the ground before he opened it.

He asked if we would help him because he was putting sheets of a newspaper—the *Miami Metropolis*, as it was called those days—[into the parachute]. He wanted us to help him pack that parachute and put all those pieces of paper so it would slide out real easy.

So, he bailed out from [the plane]. It took a long time for that plane to get that high; it didn't climb as fast as they do these days. He carried a sack of flour with one corner of it cut out, and all the way down you could see that flour coming out. By the time the flour was used up you could see him falling, then when the [parachute] opened, it was like a huge flock of birds, all those sheets of newspaper coming down.

I bet those people wondered what the heck that was.

ASSASSINATION!

I was about 15. Another idiot and I were down to see [President Franklin D.

ROBERT LAMME

Roosevelt] come in. The yacht came in and they put up the gangway, and—he, of course, was partly paralyzed from polio—they helped him into this big green Pierce-Arrow touring car. There was a big reception waiting for him down at the Bayfront Park, down at the band shell. He was to give a speech. There were lots of big-shots there, including Mayor [Anton] Cermak of Chicago. But Benny—that's my friend—and I got there and saw him get into the darned Pierce-Arrow. We jumped on the back bumper. We rode, I guess, about 50 yards on it. The Marines that were there finally pushed us off.

So we started walking down toward the band shell . . . just as we were getting even with the place to go up in the band shell, we heard what sounded like a bunch of firecrackers going off.

As it happened, my sister who is two years younger than I am, she was sitting only two rows away from [the gunman] and she saw the whole thing real close up, where everybody grabbed him.

It took [Mayor Cermak], I think, 19 days to die. These days he wouldn't have died. They didn't have any [trauma center]. It wouldn't even have been real serious.

The police kept us from getting all the way up. But we were so close, we got part way there. We didn't know for sure what had gone on. But we did see 'em come out driving, hauling [gunman] Guiseppe Zangara with them.

We was only about five feet tall.

THE ORANGE BOWL

I saw the very first [Orange Bowl]. The first one was played out at Moore Park, near 36th Street and about 10th Avenue. It was called the Festival of Palms, and that game was [between] the University of Miami and Manhattan University, which was a pretty well known school then, no real powerhouse.

Miami walked out on them 7 to 0. I still see Cecil Cook going across the goal line in the south goal. They were pretty good. I went to every Orange Bowl game until the 1953 one. But I didn't go, because the University of Miami played in the Gator Bowl then and I went to see that instead.

PAT MAY

Pat May is a general-assignment reporter for the Herald.

BY
BEA MOSS

ALICIA BARO

Real estate executive Alicia Baro has been an advocate for Dade's disfranchised for more than 40 years.

We read an article in the *Herald* [in the 1950s]. ... They showed a picture of these people sitting on a corner of North Miami Avenue and Flagler Street. ... These people had been brought from Puerto Rico to work in the camps. Because there was a freeze, and they had no job for them, they just dumped them on North Miami Avenue ... and I saw that picture and I got so furious that I decided that I was going to do something about that.

We started writing to Puerto Rico to see what we could do. We started complaining here. Naturally, there was nothing we could do because the law was what it was, and that what they had to do was stop them from coming. They couldn't be contracted. They were all classified naturally as Puerto Ricans and therefore a lot of them did not know the language. And we started visiting the camps to find out what was going on ... in South Dade.

They were charged for everything they used. The spoon, the plate, everything they were charged [for]. And in the end they would only be paid a miserable dollar or something like that.

You know they say [migrant] conditions are bad now. At that time they were unbelievable. They had outhouses. They had no place to shower. At least I remember that as we worked and protested and kept visiting the camps and kept complaining to the state attorney and the police department and whatever ... eventually down there they built these stalls where they could take showers.

I did most of the protesting, writing letters. We went before the Dade County Commission. We talked to them. We went to the City of Miami. I would be the speaker because ... I was bilingual.

As time went on, we were able to get the agency closed down. I can't remember the name of that agency that used to advertise [for workers in Puerto

ALICIA BARO

Rico]. We were able to get them to warn them not to come to Miami, because they couldn't put them on contract. You see, when you're on a contract, you are protected more. . . . Then of course the civil rights movement came, etc., and supposedly the discrimination could not be open.

My father was an idealist. My father was the type of person who protested. He spoke well and he was well versed. He knew the issues. And he would protest. He would go to the middle of the square in the little town that he was born in [in Puerto Rico] and he would protest the things that were going on in that town.

When we moved to the States he was very protective of [his] roots. He kept telling us we must not forget our language. We must not forget where we came from and who we were . . . and every time someone from Puerto Rico would write that they were coming to New York [before I moved to Miami], he would open the door. Many a person that came to New York for the first time—ventured into New York—stayed at our house, at our apartment, until he was able to get on his own, get a job, etc. He always had a door open for anybody coming in. He would help them, feed them, and you know I grew up in caring for other people.

I don't remember where I was born [in Puerto Rico]. I had never been to Puerto Rico until much later after I was married. But from [my father] I got the love of country. I got that feeling that we were one family and that we had to help each other. To me the United States was my country. . . . I had that concern for others and my father always said, you know, don't forget that we are this and we are that and he used to tell me the history of his family and how they happened and who they were. He is the one that gave me all that.

I got involved with migrants first and then, as time went on, for example, when the Cubans came in, I helped. I tried to help them as best I could. When it came to guiding or translating, when it came to helping them form groups. That is how I got involved with the Cuban community . . . I have always maintained that closeness to our Cuban friends because there is a history of Puerto Rico and Cuba. How they helped each other. Our history indicates how Puerto Rico helped [Jose] Martí and his battle for independence.

Believe me, I think there was a change [in the migrant camps]. Not only that, but a lot of the Puerto Ricans no longer come down. Now if they come they have to come with some sort of a contract because they are United States citizens and now they have to be protected. Civil rights supposedly works. So now the population there [in the camps], Puerto Rican migrants, are not as many.

We have a ministry for refugee women and children through the Methodist church. This was established 10 or 12 years ago. This ministry was established for refugee women and children, so that we could get grants from the different departments of the church to help these refugees that were coming in. First it was some of the Cubans at that time and then, as time went on, a lot of Haitians started coming in and we decided to work with those. We were trying to empower these women and their children so that they wouldn't have to go through some of the problems that I remember my Puerto Ricans went through.

We were lucky that we got a $400,000 grant from Dade County for a microenterprise project, where we are lending money to the different people. Helping to set them up in business so that they would work for themselves. And then we empower the women and give them a sense of joy and

ALICIA BARO

pride in what they are doing and get them off welfare rolls and get them off any kind of welfare they were receiving.

I tried so hard to make people aware of their rights. Make them aware that they didn't have to do this. . . . I made them aware that they could protest. They could voice their concerns. They could do all these things. But when you are in a foreign country, to them, you're afraid to protest. You feel that maybe, you know, that little fear, that intimidation. Some of them preferred leaving than making a fuss.

They eventually started to run away because they were afraid. They really were afraid. When you have a person that oversees you and that person is strong, you know, you're afraid. Especially these men coming from Puerto Rico, where everything is so different. Where there is a sense of togetherness and family, a union. And over here they would huddle with each other but they were afraid. When they came and complained to us, a group came and complained to us and brought copies of the little checks they got at the end of the week. And told us about some of the food. They couldn't eat it.

I think [such involvement] humanizes us. By that I mean people should be aware of these things. People should be involved. . . . I tell my women now, you have to know the issues. You have to know what is going on. You have to get involved in community. . . . Your community is your community. It's your neighbors. It is your family and it's you, and you have to be able to live in peace.

You are responsible for your brother, for your neighbor. You are responsible for the well-being not only of your family but of your community. I think it's the most wonderful experience that you could have, getting involved with other people, trying to help other people, trying to guide or being a mentor or whatever it is that you have to be. It's the most satisfying experience, believe me.

BEA MOSS

Bea Moss is a Herald *Neighbors reporter and columnist.*

BY
TONY PUGH

ENID PINKNEY

Enid Pinkney works to ensure that African Americans' role in Miami's history is acknowledged and preserved.

I went to Dunbar Elementary School; that wasn't too far from my house. I was at 1827 NW Fifth Court, and Dunbar was on 20th Street between Fifth Avenue and Fifth Court on 20th Street, so I could walk to school and I had very pleasant memories of going to school at Dunbar. I had teachers, good teachers; I remember them.

It was a very pleasant experience because I was in the school play when we graduated from sixth grade to Booker T. [Washington], which was a big thing. I was in the school play, and we had to learn our parts and get our costumes and we were an integral part of the school. I always was helping the teachers.

We had three bedrooms [in our home] and we had a living room and in the living room we had a piano and took music from Professor Arthur Leslie. He'd come to the house; he'd charge 25 cents a lesson—and I wish I had learned more—but he would come to your house and teach you lessons in piano. He spoke French; he also had classes on Saturday mornings. He spoke French, German and Spanish.

[He was a] black man. He was from Cat Island [in the Bahamas] and so my father knew him and my father wanted us to be under his tutelage. On Saturday mornings he had a music theory class and he taught theory at a lady's house on Fifth Avenue, and he also taught music history. I remember him teaching us about Bach and Brahms and Beethoven. I remember his class was at 6 o'clock in the morning—on Saturday. He felt that your brain was in better shape early in the morning, and he had a lot of students. The parents made them go to hear what Mr. Leslie had to say, and I still remember some of the musicians that he taught us about.... And he taught Castilian Spanish.

We were so proud of ourselves because we were

ENID PINKNEY

taught to believe in ourselves. We were somebody. We had to achieve. We had to do work in school; a lot of the problems today, I think, come from the idea of having people think of themselves [as] being poor and having poverty of spirit—and we were not given that.

The church was very influential in our lives and we expressed ourselves in church. I had to learn during the Christmas and Easter and special occasions—we had to learn a recitation. You had to commit it to memory and you had to get up there and say it and make your parents proud. You sang in the choir. You visited other churches and you had to perform. So we had the schools, the teachers believing in you. Our teachers believed that we could learn. And that was the difference. Our churches expected us to perform.

I went to the Church of God of Prophecy.... The music was so good the white people used to come from Miami Beach in these long limousines. Their chauffeurs would bring them to the church to hear the music and the preaching.

There would be so many white people in the church that they had to make room for them, and they would move the children; we had to give up our seats for these white folks to be comfortable, and they treated them so nice because, you know, they were putting money in the church. They brought a lot of money so they had to really accommodate them. Overtown was where people came, and white people were not afraid to come in Overtown.

They came to Overtown—in fact, I was talking to a white man who used to go to Miami Beach to the entertainment when the big stars would come—Josephine Baker and some of the other big stars. He told me that when he found out that they would have these jam sessions after they left places like the Fontainebleau [Hotel], they would come to Overtown for a jam session at the Sir John or maybe the Mary Elizabeth Hotel or some of the black places. He found out that they had better sessions over there than they had when he had paid all that money to go see them.

The neighborhood was intact. And these were people who had been there a long time and we knew each other. Everybody knew each other. It was like one family. And if I did something wrong and if somebody saw me, it was just like my mother seeing me.

[My parents] lived at 4609 Pine Tree Drive [in Miami Beach], because that's where they worked. They lived on what we call "premises," On the premises of the white people. And there was a servant's quarters at this address and, in fact, when my parents got married, that's where they went to live, but they had a home in Overtown. Because we were not allowed to go to school over on Miami Beach, so we had to go to Dunbar. So my grandmother came in and my aunt came in to live with us so that we would have some adults at home.

My brother was born in the servant's quarters at 4609 Pine Tree Drive. And when the doctor went to record his birth they refused to put Miami Beach on his birth certificate. Black folks were not supposed to have been born on Miami Beach. So my goal for him is to get his birth certificate straight.

OVERTOWN SHAPED US

You know, my daddy had a lot of faith and he really didn't have the money to send me to college, you know, but he believed that the Lord said, "If you make one step, you'll make two" and with the little money that he had, he sent it up there [to Talladega College in Alabama in 1949]. And he would write me letters giving me Bible scriptures to read.

In 1955 [when I returned to Miami] Overtown was pretty much

ENID PINKNEY

the same. I got a job working at Dorsey Junior High School, teaching there and I didn't have a car so I would catch the bus, 21 bus, and go to Liberty City to teach.... I taught English.

The social life was still intact but it was later on when people started moving out.... They had us thinking that it was a slum area. You know, the government, and they were going to make things better.

Back then, we, my parents, did not fight for our neighborhoods. We believed what they told us. That is, it was a slum neighborhood and that they were going to make it better. Urban renewal came through. And you know, I haven't seen that come to pass yet. And then also around that time the expressway [Interstate 95] was coming through.

The expressway was coming through and then it was like, "You better get out or sell your property because the value is going to go down."... But then there were some people who had made some pretty good money so they were moving out, not because of either one of those; they just wanted to move into what you would call a better neighborhood.... That would have been [to the Liberty City area], or to Richmond Heights or to Orchard Villa. Some were coming out here to Brownsville.

I still feel ties to Overtown. And I still talk about Overtown, because I get very upset when people talk negatively about Overtown, because then I know that they really don't understand the Overtown that I grew up in.... We failed the place that gave us what we had. The reason that we are what we are today is because of the values that we found in Overtown, because of the families, of the caring neighborhoods, the caring teachers, the caring churches, the love that people —you know, we had something.

TONY PUGH

Tony Pugh is a Herald *reporter.*

BY ROSA BAUTISTA

DRS. PEDRO JOSE GREER

Dr. Pedro Jose Greer Sr. and his son, Dr. Joe Greer Jr., are gastroenterologists. They share a practice and a tradition of helping the needy.

Father: My first impression of Miami after we arrived at the airport [from Cuba in 1944] was what now is 36th Street. It looked to me like those Texas towns you used to see in the movies: isolated, no large buildings. Almost every house was a one-story building. The airport was relatively small; it was not considered to be an international airport.

The Hispanic population was very small. South Americans and Puerto Ricans made up the bulk of the community; there were very few Cubans, very few.

Life in Miami was free, tranquil. Security on the streets was remarkable; you could leave your car unlocked and not worry about your personal property. The crime rate was minimal, compared with today. The biggest concern was [World War II], so everything was related to the end of the war and what would happen afterward.

If you traveled from Miami to Hollywood, there would be a 10- to 15-mile stretch of open land. Nowadays, Miami, Hollywood and Fort Lauderdale are practically one continuous city. Miami's outward spread was slow but constant.

We stayed in Miami until 1950. I finished college and returned to Cuba to study medicine.... My last year in college, I moved to Spain and graduated there. My degree was issued in Madrid. In 1957, we moved to Miami. [By 1979] Joey was in college. When he finished college, he told me he wanted to become a doctor. He spoke very poor Spanish at the time.

Son: At that time, there weren't that many Cubans in Miami, so we wanted to speak English. We wanted to have blue eyes, blond hair and be surfers. That was America to me.

Father: He resented having the other school kids treat him as "a Cuban."

Son: If you spoke Spanish in school, you got detention. You were not allowed to speak Spanish

DRS. PEDRO JOSE GREER

in school. That was up until the early 1970s. I was also taught that, if a single person didn't speak the language, you'd speak a language all would understand, as a courtesy.

Father: When Joey decided to take up medicine, he made plans to study in a Latin American country where he could study medicine and brush up on Spanish. He kept saying he wanted to leave Miami; he would finish his school and go west to treat the Indians, or to Africa, to take care of the poor.

He left for Santo Domingo [in the Dominican Republic] when he was 22. When he finished his studies in Santo Domingo, three years later, he got married.

Son: I lived there six years.

Father: He wanted to go to a Third World country, but luckily when he started training here in Miami he realized that this city had a Third World country within. He finished school in 1984.

Son: In 1962, we moved to Westchester, to an all-Jewish neighborhood. We were the first Cubans there. At that time, 97th Avenue was as far west as you went.... On Coral Way and 97th Avenue, there were strawberry fields. We used to walk through the fields and for a quarter, we got a small basket of strawberries, 35 cents for a big basket. The TV series "Gentle Ben" was made right down the street.... There was a sign outside our house that said, "End of World, Two Miles."

Father: He learned from his mother that he should take care of his friends. His house was his friends' house. What his mother wanted was for him to feel comfortable, because she didn't want him to leave the house.

Son: My friends would come in when no one was at home, make food, and leave notes telling my mother what to buy. "You need more bread, more ham...."

Father: When Joey started work on Camillus [House], a reporter from a Catholic newspaper wanted to get an idea about [my wife] Nenita and I, and how Joey picked up the idea of being kind to the needy. She said, "He must have been a very docile youngster, with a deep feeling for religion." All I could say was, "Not really."

Son: I grew up in a city that grew up at the same time I did. I was able to see Miami from a kid's perspective, from the end of an old era, where you could go across the street and play with a cow, to walking under bridges and seeing people smoke crack.

All of a sudden, Miami became the city of our generation. I remember Frankie Varona, a good friend of mine; his mother is archivist for the Cuban Museum at the University of Miami. I remember when Frankie became a U.S. citizen. We couldn't call him Francisco anymore; we had to call him Frankie.

The times were different. The issues of discipline were different. As a kid in junior high I used to get goose bumps when I heard the Pledge of Allegiance or "The Star-Spangled Banner."

Father: Joey sets himself a goal and does everything in his power to reach it. In his mind, obstacles will not interfere with his quest for whatever he's seeking. You can't imagine how many obstacles he had while creating Camillus. He used to think, "Everybody is going to help me," but that wasn't the case.

Son: You must understand the politics of medicine and what I call the politics of poverty. Some people think they have a monopoly over treatment of the poor. You might think there's gold involved in this. At the beginning, I became a threat to some people. We were never taught about poverty but we were expected to treat poor people.

Father: Joey has all the qualifications, but dedication is the most important.

Son: I get that from you. Medicine is an art balanced by

DRS. PEDRO JOSE GREER

science. No disease comes alone; all diseases come with people. It's a matter of holding somebody's hand or listening.

When you're with a patient, you listen. You hold his or her hand, touch him. These are human beings, they have feelings. The same thing with the homeless and poor. Nobody has ever listened to them. If I walk in there and a homeless man starts cursing me, why should I be mad? I have a nice tie, a nice shirt, an air-conditioned car, I'm not living on the streets. He doesn't know who I am or what my intentions are. So it's my responsibility to sit back and listen.

The reason we go under the bridges—and I don't do that very often; I used to go once or twice a week, now I do it once a month—is very simple. Not to treat people under the bridge, but to get them to trust you enough to come to the clinic.

Why would they want to come in? You have to prove to them: "Look, we're for real. Come on in. We're here to take care of you." If someone says, "I'm a crack addict," I'm not going to say, "It's bad to be a crack addict." I'll say, "When you're ready to have some help, come down to the clinic. We'll take care of you."

Medicine is to serve people. The reality is, it's fun; it's fun to be a doctor. I have a distant uncle who works at one of the HMOs, high up. When I was growing up, my mom and dad gave these parties, and there were doctors like Otto García, an extraordinary pediatrician. He and my dad would tell me how great medicine is—they said they would never retire, the day they stopped practice they would take care of the poor—this is what I grew up with.

Then I had another distant uncle, a doctor too, and he'd sit by the bar with a drink in his hand and he'd say, "It's all bullshit." And I'm sitting there, thinking, "Which one do I want to be like?"

ROSA BAUTISTA-TOWNSEND

Rosa Bautista-Townsend is a reporter for El Nuevo Herald. Renato Perez translated this interview.

BY
CARL HIAASEN

SUSIE JIM BILLIE

At 95, Susie Jim Billie is one of the oldest members of the Seminole Tribe, an elder and medicine woman. She lives at the Big Cypress Reservation near Immokalee. In the accompanying photograph, she is wearing a traditional Seminole dress that she made.

Q: Where were you born?

I was born in the Everglades near where the Miccosukees live today on the [Tamiami] Trail. We lived in chickees. A platform was built inside, for a bed.

Q: Tell me a little about your mother and father.

There weren't any jobs. There were people who bought and traded pelts near the Everglades. Dad hunted and sold the hides. Mom tanned the hides. Deer meat was popular, so my parents made jerky and sold it. That's how we bought other food.

Food was real cheap back then. Grits were 50 cents. Sugar was cheap, corned beef was 25 cents. Material for clothing was 10 cents a yard.

Q: Did your father hunt from a dugout canoe?

They hunted on foot because a lot of the area was dry land. He hunted alligators, raccoons, otters, all mostly on foot.

Q: Are your memories of these times happy ones?

My childhood, yes, it was happy. I think about my parents when they used to plant corn, squash, and have a garden. We all helped pick the vegetables. It was the good days. Now food costs lots of money. We don't grow gardens anymore.

Q: Do you remember the first white man you ever saw?

I first saw them at the Chokoloskee Store, a trading store near Everglades City. We traded and sold deer meat with the people at the store. A lot of people came in canoes to trade or shop—if not canoes, the people traveled in buggies with cows called oxen.

Back then we traded with them and socialized with them often. Some white people even learned some of the [Seminole] language. Both groups of people respected each other and got along. They were good people, back then.

Q: Do you remember

SUSIE JIM BILLIE

hearing stories about the wars with the white man?

My mother's mother said she remembered running with her two uncles from the soldiers. She was little. Her uncles got killed.

She remembered she cried and cried during the time they were running. The family told her to be quiet, so the soldiers wouldn't hear them.

Q: Can you remember the hurricanes?

Yes, I remember very well. Our people always knew when the hurricanes were coming. We would build a special chickee with very short legs. The chickee was like a lean-to.

We would build the chickee in thick palmetto patches or brush, take food in there, and stay until the hurricane passed.

Q: There were no weather reports back then. How did you know when the hurricane was coming?

We knew signs from the clouds, different changes in the sky. We observed other signs, like certain berries or plants grew during the hurricane season. Some hurricanes were hard and bad—it would break a lot of pine trees. That's why we never built the chickee in piney areas.

Our people used Indian medicine during this time to help protect us from the bad storm. We had chants to try to make the hurricane go around us.

Q: When did you learn the medicine?

I wasn't young, but I don't remember the exact age. I was taught by my family to learn as much as possible, so I can help people who might need it in the future. I learned it along with my brothers and sisters and aunts and uncles.

It is a long process of training, but back then we didn't have all the distractions like today. So we learned pretty fast.

Q: When is the first time you saw television?

I knew there was television around because people were talking about it, watching it. When I finally saw one, I got dizzy and it made me ill. So I didn't watch it anymore, until recently.

I had an experience one time—this was worse! There was a big movie house in Everglades City. I went to it. I sat there and got sick to my stomach. I got dizzy. I ran outside and found a palm tree and fell down beside it. I thought I was dying!

Q: Do you remember your first automobile ride?

I was well up in age when I rode in my first automobile. Maybe I might have been in my 50s, I don't know.

I like the car. You get there a little faster.

Q: What's the farthest place from the Everglades that you've ever been?

I went to Washington, D.C. It was about eight years ago. It was my first airplane ride, the only time. I liked the plane. [She had been asked to come to the Library of Congress and help identify tape recordings of old medicine chants.]

Q: What's the biggest change that you've seen in the Seminole culture, since you were a child?

Children back then were well behaved. Families lived together well. They had camps. Each camp took care of their own. Everyone helped with the upbringing of their children. Children respected more things, cared more for others' well-being. The family structure was better back then. Now families are more split up.

Q: When you were young, did you often go to Miami?

When I was little, we didn't spend much time in the city. We stayed pretty much in the Everglades. When I got older we went to Miami.

I didn't care too much about [going to] the city, but I liked the oxen ride. That was fun.

SUSIE JIM BILLIE

Q: What are your best memories?

My good memories are with my family. Things that made me happy were the teachings from my parents—like cooking, gardening, and especially learning the herbal medicine.

We used to grow a lot of corn. We roasted it. We made a drink called *sofkee*.

Q: What are some of the sad memories?

When I lost my father it was the saddest. He was the strongest one. Then I lost my mother, and that was very sad.

I've lost some children of my own, which was hard.

Q: How do you feel about all the changes that have occurred in the part of Florida that you know, and grew up in?

It was better back then, not so crowded, fewer people. [Today there are] too many distractions that keep people from learning things. Now too much is going on at the same time, not enough peace and quiet.

Q: How have the Everglades changed?

There were a lot of animals—bears, deer, panthers. We ate the bears and deer. Once in a while we killed a panther. We used panthers only for medicine purposes. We didn't waste things, we only took things when we needed it for a purpose—whether food or spiritual. Today the animals aren't as abundant.

Q: What are your hopes for your family?

I had eight children. I have two living today. I have 26 grandchildren, 41 great-grandchildren, and nine great great-grandchildren.

I don't think too much about the future of the grandkids. I hope they all do well. I worry about one son, who has Down's syndrome. [I worry] how he'll be when I pass on.

I hope everyone is successful and happy even when I'm gone. I try not to think negative thoughts too much about my family, for it makes me sad. I want good for all my grandchildren, and their children.

(photo by Tim Chapman)

CARL HIAASEN

Carl Hiaasen is a novelist and a columnist for the Herald. *Susie Jim Billie speaks a Seminole dialect. Her interview was translated by her granddaughter, Jeanette Cypress.*